THE QUEST FOR FREEDOM

The Quest for Freedom

Belgian Resistance in World War II

YVONNE de RIDDER FILES

FITHIAN PRESS
SANTA BARBARA • 1991

Design and typography by Jim Cook

Published by Fithian Press
Post Office Box 1525
Santa Barbara, California 93102

LIBRARY OF CONGRESS CATALGOGING-IN-PUBLICATION DATA
Files, Yvonne, 1913–
    The quest for freedom: the life of a Belgian resistance fighter / Yvonne
Files
      p.   cm.
    ISBN 0-931832-93-4
    1. Files, Yvonne, 1913– . 2. World War, 1939–1945—Underground
movements-Belgium. 3. World War, 1939–1945—Personal narratives,
Belgian. 4. Guerrillas—Belgium—Biography. 5. Belgium—History—
German occupation, 1940–1945. I. Title.
D802.B4F55   1991
940.53'37'092—dc 20
[b]   91-17025
                                                                CIP

Contents

To all whose love
and defense of Country
helped bring back freedom.

Part One:
Invasion

1 On Friday, 10 May 1940, we in Antwerp, Belgium, were awakened at 4:45 A.M. by the rumbling sound of aircraft overhead. Not an unusual occurrence, because of the German Luftwaffe's flights over the territory on their way to bomb England, with whom they had been officially at war since the German invasion of Poland in September 1939.

This time, however, it seemed different; there was an eerie feeling, then apprehension, when the firing of the Belgian anti-aircraft batteries increased. Dawn of this balmy new day unveiled nothing unusual in the sky above, and we went back to bed. But a moment later the anti-aircraft fire started anew in full force. We ran through the apartment, scanning the sky from every window, in every direction, and spotted five German airplanes surrounded by the anti-aircraft explosions. Then the sky seemed to fill with aircraft coming from diverse directions. We thought this was a German mass attack on England in process. At that moment we counted about forty aircraft at high altitude, while others in smaller groups were flying at a lower level in the opposite direction.

Then suddenly the characteristic whistle of a bomb, followed by the deflagration and smoke. This sequence increased, as did the fire from the anti-aircraft batteries.

If anyone had any doubt as to the reality of the situation, it was very soon dispelled by the announcement on Belgian Radio, that "during the night the Germans invaded Holland, Belgium, and Luxembourg"; that we were at war with Germany, and had appealed to the Allies for help.

The events moved at a fast pace. The bombing increased. The port area seemed to be one of the selected areas, and the tunnel under the Scheldt River in particular. The tunnel was the direct link to the main highway to the Flanders and the North Sea beaches.

The Belgian reservists were called back; all were to rejoin their units. Among the civilian population, the exodus was starting as well.

Panic, fear, and apprehension are food for paranoia, creating some sad, unfortunate incidents which, in retrospect, have a touch of humor. Parachutists were "seen" everywhere. Very often correctly so, but the "sighting" near my father's home (where we were presently spending the nights) was not. The brouhaha, the shouting, and the melee were caused by the apprehension of two supposed parachutists, who were beaten up and turned over to the authorities. It turned out one of them was a French soldier and the other was a citizen of Antwerp!

Many sightings of spies and parachutists in the following days were, indeed, genuine. One day I came upon a "nun" over six feet tall, walking with a stride that was far from feminine. I followed the "nun," noticing other characteristics, only to suddenly have "her" vanish after turning the corner! The habit was a common disguise.

The bombing increased, the advance of the German armies accelerated, and the port of Antwerp became their main objective.

Segments of the population who had experienced German occupation during World War I were understandably very apprehensive. And the exodus increased.

Several members of my husband's family left on the third day; other friends had left or were going. On the fifth day, my husband, Ed, who was American born and carried a foreign identity card, started being gripped by "the fear." It was understandable that he should be afraid, the more so as he was of Jewish descent.

During the night of May 15 the rumbling we heard all night long was not that of the Luftwaffe bombings, but of the cannon fire of the approaching German Army. Ed wanted to leave at all cost. There was no way of holding him back, and although I felt heartbroken at the thought of fleeing, I didn't let on; I felt it was my duty to my husband to do as he wished.

By this time, transportation of any kind out of the city had become nearly impossible. Cars, taxis, and trucks, were streaming out of town. The roads were already clogged, and no more vehicles were available.

At daybreak we walked toward downtown, trying in vain to find a ride, and finally came back home around 8 A.M. There, an opportunity presented itself. A neighbor mentioned that her son was leaving in the morning; he already had two truckloads full of people, but she thought he could find a place for us as well! My heart sank; as much as I understood Ed's fear, I myself hated to flee. I felt like a coward. But my place was with him, of course, and three hours later we embarked on a truck with fifteen other people, including a small boy, the driver, and the owner of the truck.

2 At 11 A.M., after showing our identity cards to the soldiers and gendarmes posted near the entrance to the tunnel under the Scheldt River, we were authorized to leave the city, and our exodus started, direction Ghent.

The scenery along the highways would be repeated daily during our pilgrimage: long, interminable lines of cars, trucks, and all types of vehicles creeping along at a snail's pace. Interspersed among them were people on foot silently pushing carts or carrying heavy loads on their backs or in their arms, and bicyclists young and old, and even the infirm. This vision seemed unreal for the horror and the pain it instilled.

On the outskirts of Deynze, where we stopped for a bite to eat, there was suddenly a big agitation: there were people on the road running and pointing up toward the sky, where a German parachutist was floating down, protected by a German plane circling above him. Belgian soldiers took off in pursuit, hoping to apprehend this "spy" or "saboteur."

At the outskirts of Menin, not far from the French border, we saw our first "Tommies"—British soldiers—directing traffic. We saluted them with the thumbs-up sign, which they returned with enthusiasm. Our first detour—the first of many—occurred here; we were not permitted to take the route to Ypres. Soon we crossed the French border, and by 6:45 P.M. we stopped at Armentières. The inhabitants were most kind, offering lodging and trying to help in every way.

Our leader, Mr. Pitoors, had already arranged lodging for the group, a total of thirty-seven people. It was a big meeting room on the first floor of a café. In our group were five or six children, the youngest six months old. Following the advice of the leader's sister-in-law, we accepted the offer of an old lady to pass the night in her home. This lady even insisted we use her own bedroom.

It was a clean home; the bedroom filled with a myriad of bibelots: hundreds of keepsakes—photos, ceramics, etc.—accumulated over a long period. We sank into the soft bed, wondering what tomorrow had in store.

Our awakening the next morning was exciting! A big, brown flat bug, the size of one's little fingernail, was moving gingerly across the top sheet, just a few inches from our faces! Although I have a horror of squashing any insect, I folded over the sheet and pressed hard. When I opened the fold, our visitor took off as fast as he could, unharmed! I mounted a second attack, and then a third, when I finally did hit the head—obviously the only vulnerable part. As you may have guessed, it was a bedbug, called in French *punaise,* which translates in English as "thumb-tack." A very appropriate name!

We jumped out of bed, fearful that some of the bugs might have found refuge in our luggage or clothes, for they are renowned for their prolific reproduction!

We joined the other members of our group for a cup of coffee before starting on the next leg of our journey. We pondered over the reports given to us the previous night just before retiring, by remnants of a *Chasseurs Ardennais* contingent. They were worn out, having sustained the brunt of the first German onslaught near Namur. The German Luftwaffe had strafed them in their trenches, flying at near ground level. The *Chasseurs* had also been the target of a tank corps attack, and hadn't had the weapons to defend themselves against such a force. They had also watched a mass of parachutists coming down ahead of their lines. When they charged, they discovered that these "parachutists" were dummies; the real men had then dropped behind the lines, and mowed them down as they returned toward their positions. There were 10 men remaining of a company of 200, and 19 of a company of 240. A train had evacuated another group of 150 the preceding day.

Our journey continued ever deeper into France. The search for food and drink became more and more arduous; the gasoline became rarer and rarer as well. We spent night after night in barns, sometimes offered by the farmers, sometimes abandoned by their owners. In a group like ours there is bound to be tension, and there is bound to be a troublemaker, one who is never satisfied, and who always knows better, and who is eternally ungrateful. And we were not spared! We did have one such character amongst us.

Saturday, our third day on the road, we experienced the anxiety of being strafed when a German fighter appeared at tree-level, blasting its machine guns. Everyone had jumped out of the stopped column and into the ditch on the side of the road. One poor cow in the pasture adjacent to the road was apparently the only casualty.

The column seemed completely bogged down, so our trucks turned off into a dirt side-road. It was such a contrast there: so quiet, like a different world. Not a sound except the crackling of the tires rolling over thousands and thousands of June bugs, which literally formed a thick carpet on the road. I had never seen such a sight!

At the end of this arbor, we found ourselves in a clearing bordered by two big, seemingly brand-new barns. No one was around. There was a water well. The whole group bedded down for the night on the fresh straw, all, that is, but my husband and me. We were very wary of the fleas, and we stretched out instead in the truck on top of several suitcases of all forms and dimensions, trying to have some shut-eye.

This was to be a forced halt; both cars were out of gas, and hope of finding any was dim. However, two of the men went off on gasoline detail while the rest of us started pulling up buckets of water from the well. It was Sunday, May 19, our fourth day. It seemed we had been on the go for weeks.

As we finally sat down on the grass to have a bite to eat from our provisions, a familiar rumbling approached. Planes overhead! The trucks were hastily pushed deep under the trees, and all of us hid under the green canopy nature provided us. There was a fear that these two big hangers might be mistaken by the Germans as military barracks, and thus subjected to bombing. The planes—six of them—circled, but went on without attacking. Toward dark there was a second similar alert but no attack.

Monday found us in Rouen, where complete pandemonium reigned. Traffic was at a complete standstill. In this mass of humanity, we ran into several acquaintances.

Thursday, May 23, our eighth day, would be our last on the road. That day we arrived in Poitiers, which turned out to have become

Exodus

ANTWERP TO POITIERS

the center for the regrouping of several Belgian governmental departments, officials, etc. Although the rest of the group decided to go on toward Toulouse, we chose to disembark and take our chances there.

Luck was with us. Through the auspices of one of the employees at the prefecture where we had to report and inquire as to possibilities of lodging, we were put in contact with a couple of retired teachers. They were charming people; he was a veteran of World War I. They offered to let us stay either with them in their home here in town, or in a room they had on the outskirts of town. Mrs. Vaudeleau advised us to go and have a look there, and was convinced we would opt for it immediately!

This "room" turned out to be a delightful little villa with a lovely bedroom, a big room which was the dining room, a little veranda, and a small hothouse on the side of the building. All of this was surrounded by a big garden! We couldn't believe our eyes, and accepted their generous offer immediately, expressing our thanks and enthusiasm to Mr. Vaudeleau, who had driven us to the location.

We got back to the truck in town, took our belongings off the truck, thanked Mr. Pitoors for having taken us along, and wished the rest of the party good luck. They were all going on. One was only allowed to stay in Poitiers if one could find lodging; otherwise one had to continue toward the departments reserved for Belgian refugees further toward southern France. Poitiers was, as mentioned before, overcrowded with Belgian refugees, and there was no lodging to be found. We were among the privileged ones!

3 During our stay in Poitiers, from May 24 to August 9, the kindness of our hosts was incredible. They became like our adoptive parents. We shared with them the shame of the capitulation of the Belgian Army, ordered by King Leopold on May 28. History, of course, proved there was no way the Belgian Army could have withstood the German onslaught, even with the help of the French and British soldiers who had poured into the country. However, the unforgivable act of capitulating before advising our allies of our intention was criminal, for it caused the unforgivable entrapment of the British and French troops.

Poitiers was teeming with Belgian government officials, judicial personalities, etc., many of them friends or professional relations of my father. But none could give me any news of Father. We had learned in the meantime that Ed's relatives were all safe, some back home in Antwerp, others further south in France.

Ed got in contact with several personalities in hopes of finding a job. (Our financial reserve was rather meager.) This, however, proved to be hopeless for both my husband and myself. The situation in France continued to deteriorate; the German advance was relentless. Ed's desire to go to America was growing.

Ed was advised of possible employment in Bordeaux. The journey on the train—which he took alone—was terrible. The train was repeatedly halted to let military trains carrying personnel or ammunition go by, and Ed arrived in Bordeaux ten hours late. The job offer was a "misunderstanding."

Ed took advantage of being in Bordeaux to visit the American consulate there, and was appalled by the "bureaucratic" mind that prevailed there. He inquired as to the possibility of returning to America, for he was American born; I, however, being a Belgian citizen, first needed two American witnesses whose signatures had to be legalized in America then returned to Bordeaux. In a place and time where every hour—every minute—counted, this bureaucracy seemed incongruous!

Sunday, June 16, the exodus picked up momentum. On this main road (Poitiers-Châteauroux) in front of our residence, we saw an unending defile of cars packed to the gills, and innumerable bicycle riders. This time they were French citizens, all fleeing south.

At the home of our benefactors we heard on the radio that the ministers had had a meeting, and that Paul Reynaud would make an announcement.

In the afternoon of this Sunday, the trucks from the INR (Institut National de Radiodiffusion) Belgian Radio, which had been parked since May 25 one hundred yards from our house, were packing and preparing to leave. The Belgian ministerial offices were leaving as well. All these were bad omens. Rumors were flying. A French soldier proclaimed that Marshal Pétain, the World War I hero who had formed a new cabinet with General Weygand as minister of defense, had made a radio announcement that he had asked Hitler to stipulate his peace conditions. No one could conceive that such a request would come from Marshall Pétain. Alas, the news was confirmed. The hostilities would stop.

The following morning, however, at 6 A.M., the sirens wailed and the alert remained in effect until 7:30. The hostilities were not halted during the negotiations.

Food was becoming much scarcer. Ever since the influx of Parisians, one had had to stand in line in front of the bakeries whose doors remained closed until the bread was baked. But now, eggs, butter, cheese, and other staples became a rarity.

Official announcements were pasted on the walls advising that no one was allowed to leave the city and that those who tried would be turned back.

On Wednesday, June 19, the Germans began bombing Poitiers, about 11:30 A.M. in the direction of Châteauroux; then, at 3:20 P.M., Poitiers itself. We didn't see any airplanes, but black smoke was billowing from the town, and successive explosions filled the air. We learned later that the train station had been hit, an ammunition train the obvious target.

On the radio it was announced that the French plenipotentiaries had arrived at the front and had made contact with the German authorities.

A French soldier arriving from Tours, where he was in charge of bridge demolition, reported that Tours had offered a strong defense. The French troops had been forced to retreat, and had blown up the big stone bridge as they withdrew. The Germans had arrived in

Tours yesterday morning, and the Loire River was now the barrier to their advance.

Although the heavy traffic had subsided yesterday, today it started anew. But this time it consisted mainly of military traffic—trucks filled with French soldiers, and a whole column of cannons.

Suddenly, in rapid succession, four bombs exploded. The roar of the airplane engines became audible only a short while later, but the plane remained hidden from view in the clouds above. Some explosions further in the distance followed; then we heard nothing. A few minutes later the farmer, our neighbor, excitedly called out that he just "saw the plane at 200 feet!" I thought I had misunderstood, but just then a twin-engine plane appeared at roof-level headed right toward us from the far end of the garden. We slammed the shutters closed and dived behind the bed, holding the bolster over our heads. The plane roared over the roof, let loose with machine-gun bursts, and was gone. I will never forget that sight: the big black plane looked as if it were going to come right through the house!

There was still no news regarding the negotiations, and the rumors were that the Germans were only seventeen kilometers from Poitiers. In the morning paper the mayor of Poitiers made an appeal for calm and order. Not a good sign!

By Saturday, June 22, there was still no decision resulting from the negotiations. According to the radio, the meeting had taken place in the Forest of Compiègne, in the same train compartment where the 1918 Armistice was signed. The French delegation was reported to be presided over by General Huntziger. The other members were Mr. Leon Noël, French ambassador, Admiral Luc, General Parisot, and the Air Force General Bergeret. The German plenipotentiaries were Hitler, Rudolf Hess, von Ribbentrop, General von Keitel, and General Brauchitch.

The first German elements arrived at the prefecture in Poitiers on June 22. Here on the outskirts of town it resembled a dead city. Not a soul was on the streets, all the shutters were closed and most of the shops also closed their doors.

I had to get some bread, and started the long walk toward the bakery. One lonely man passed by and mumbled, "Are you going to greet the Germans in town?" A few minutes later my heart sank when two German soldiers riding a side-car roared by. These were the first enemy soldiers I had seen!

The radio announced that the armistice had been signed. Talks were in progress today with Italy, and hostilities would stop six hours after Italy notified Germany that the armistice had been signed between her and France. Pierre Laval had been named ministre d'état.

The unending lines of cars passed by us again, but this time in the opposite direction. Even Belgian cars were heading back toward home.

In the following days the "occupier" tightened his grip on the population. Curfews were in effect, and weapons of all kinds were to be turned in by the citizens. Food was getting scarcer and scarcer; by June 30 no more eggs, butter, meat, potatoes, or beer were to be found. Even charcoal was unavailable, and it was announced that in two days there would be no more gas. So, what about cooking?

4 On Sunday, June 30, the Comité d'Action des Réfugiés Belges à Poitiers (Action Committee of the Belgian Refugees in Poitiers) was born with the sole aim of organizing a train for repatriation. My husband and I were both very active in the committee, he as treasurer-accountant, and I doing the secretarial work.

Frustration, disappointment, and a feeling of hopelessness were daily occurrences. Trains were only going as far as Tours, about 75 miles north; the Tours-Paris leg (150 miles) was out. Another day, the Germans forbade the crossing of the Loire River, thus keeping us pinned down in Poitiers. Day after day complications seemed to accumulate, and our hopes dwindled. The mass of Belgians didn't show understanding; some seemed to blame us, the Committee, for the delay.

To this was added the personal worries about our own families. During those several weeks we had finally established contact with my husband's family, but still I was without word from or about my father, Frédéric de Ridder. Despite the many officials, friends of my father, whom I encountered, and the several missives I had given to them for possible delivery by one means or another, no news had reached me. But finally, on July 12, word came that he was safe and well and at home.

The promise to obtain our train remained just that—a promise. A group of refugees from south of Poitiers did embark there, yesterday we were told, but under terrible conditions: they traveled in cattle cars, with no certainty of reaching Paris. Furthermore, the Royal Air Force (RAF) was reported to be attacking several points which would be on our route.

The president of the Committee would go to Paris by mail train to find out what was holding up the permission for our train. The next day, July 19, we were notified that the Germans would put a train at our disposal on Monday, July 22, at 9:30 P.M.! But this wonderful news was completely shattered the following day, when a telegram from the German authorities announced the suspension of all departures for Belgium and beyond!

The Committee's president returned on Monday, July 22, bushed. The news he brought back was far from encouraging. There were no trains between Paris and Brussels. While he was in Paris he could hear the allied bombings on the outskirts of town, and one night the anti-aircraft was active in Paris itself.

Today our blockage was confirmed, an announcement being displayed at the *Kommandatur* that all departures for Paris had been suspended.

Finally, on August 2, the German stationmaster called from Bordeaux stating that we had permission to organize our train. The following day the *Feldkommandant* in Poitiers confirmed the authorization. We supposedly would depart on Friday, August 9, at 9:30 P.M.

The weather turned hot.

It seemed as though we had been here in Poitiers for ages, although at the time of departure it would only amount to two and a half months. But there had been so many anxieties of all kinds: the present, the future, the family, and, of course, the daily search for food—practically a minor problem by comparison—which made it seem so much longer. I was carrying an additional burden. My place, of course, was at my husband's side; I hadn't hesitated one moment when he decided to leave Belgium. But still I felt ashamed to have fled. To flee was contrary to my nature, and it gnawed constantly at my conscience. Now the prospect of returning to my country was exhilarating!

When departure came and we embarked, it seemed practically unreal. Maybe we had been numbed by the seemingly eternal succession of permissions and cancellations which had been going on for days.

Then the steam engine of the locomotive puffed, the train shook, and we were on our way.

The rhythm of the wheels practically lulled us into a feeling of abandon, albeit with a slight pang of apprehension, pulling on the fringes. Suddenly the brakes screeched and the train stopped. It was dark. The adrenalin surged upward. Were the enemy troops stopping us? Would we have to back up and return to our point of departure? All sorts of thoughts and fears streaked through our minds. Then, just as suddenly, the locomotive surged forward with what seemed one final effort. The wheels turned ever so slightly, literally inch by inch, and then we heard the frightening sound of creaking lumber at each inch of forward motion. We were crossing the Loire River on the makeshift bridge stretched high above it. It was a real nightmare. We held our breath as if to make ourselves lighter. Not a word was spoken during what seemed an eternity. When finally the locomotive reached the other side with its load of passenger compartments, our emotions released, and tears and laughter exploded among the passengers.

We were told we were the first train to cross the makeshift bridge.

5 The return home was practically anti-climactic. We had experienced so many anxieties, so many hopes had been shattered
and revived; and now so many unknowns were lying ahead, so
many dangers in our path in the days, months—and who knew at
this time—years ahead.

The reunion with my father was very emotional. Here I must lay
bare, in a concise manner, our family situation. I lost my mother
when I was six years old. My father was a volunteer in World War I,
and was gone for four years, from 1914 to 1918. When he returned,
Mother, who had literally deprived herself of everything to feed me,
was reduced to skin and bones, whereas I was a healthy butterball.

I remember my father's return from the war in 1918. It was a very
emotional scene. The doorbell rang and my mother dispatched me
to answer it. A gentleman was standing there, and at the curb stood a
horse carriage with luggage. The gentleman smiled, and asked me if
Mother was home. "Yes, sir" was my answer, and before I could
turn to run and call her, there she was, running down the hallway
and falling into the arms of this stranger.

We all three walked to the drawing room, and mother, pointing
to the huge portrait of my father on the day of their wedding, asked
me if I didn't recognize who this gentleman was. When mother said,
"Darling, don't you recognize your daddy?" I was even more
perplexed. How could this full-bearded man be the same as this
clean-shaven dad in the portrait?

Their happiness was, unfortunately, of short duration. Mother
couldn't recover from her weakened condition. Instead, her health
deteriorated, and eight months later she died.

One year later my father remarried, unfortunately to the wrong
person. If he had only been able to marry the sister of this individual,
I would have been the happiest little girl in the world, but instead my
stepmother turned out to be a terrible individual who was bent to
turn my father against me. During my childhood years I knew only
punishments, from beatings to daily deprivations, all caused by lies

21

that this woman told my father. As a teenager the treatment continued, resulting in undeserved public humiliations, etc. However, due to my strictly disciplined upbringing, I never rebelled, believing this was my fate, although it was caused by such incredible injustice.

I was twenty-one years old when I left my parents' home to get married. Shortly after my marriage I was shocked to learn that my father's friends were all aware of what was happening. When I, in disbelief, asked this friend, whom I called "Uncle Henry," why he or the others had never faced my father with this, the answer was, "To what avail? You know your father!" Maybe it is the revelation of their knowing that caused me to blurt out my revolt, during the first year of World War II.

Father had come to visit me (I lived alone in my own apartment at that time), and at a certain moment, he expressed a complaint about something I supposedly had done. The way he said it, and the subject of the remark itself left no doubt as to who had instigated the reproach.

I blurted out, "*She* has sent you, hasn't she?" This was the first time I dared revolt in the sixteen years I had been subjected to all the abuse. My father was taken aback, and started his usual reaction. I stopped him in his tracks, and cried out the accumulated despair of the daily injustices I had suffered during all those years. He was flabbergasted, and in a whisper, with tears in his eyes, holding me tight, said, "Why didn't you ever tell me?" I could have reminded him then how often, when he was beating me, chasing me to my bedroom, I cried out, "I didn't do it," only for him to shout back: "Would you call your mother a liar?"

For a while after that—about six months I would say—Father's attitude toward her was cold and abrupt. But soon she took over again. She had only few occasions anymore to do me harm, until the last year of the Nazi occupation of Antwerp.

She did, however, manage to rob me of two-thirds of my mother's inheritance by forcing my father to deduct from this inheritance the expenses for the upkeep of the three-story house in which I had lived from my sixth to my twenty-first birthday! Greed had become her main occupation. None of my father's old-time friends ever understood the hold she had over him. She had no intellect—an asset which meant so much to my father, and she had no physical beauty. My father—who obviously didn't find happiness with her, had a lady-friend who shared with him his intellectual interests. They carried on their relationship for twenty-seven years before my stepmother discovered it.

How was it possible that my father, who was feared by so many, was putty in the hands of my stepmother and came to be turned against me? His employees, for instance, shook in their boots when they heard him come back at the end of the day after having visited his clients.

To make the picture complete, I should mention that my stepsister was obviously a chip off her mother's block. She was mean, deceptive, and a liar, without any moral values. Thanks to these two individuals, I could write a book about my life under their reign, entitled *The Modern Cinderella*.

Now, back in Antwerp, the first big change for us was to find less expensive quarters. With the uncertainty of financial survival hanging over our heads, a drastic cut was necessary. From our spacious apartment we moved to a much smaller one a few blocks away, and then faced the daily struggle of survival.

I continued to work for my father as his secretary. It was a very demanding job, and he was a very demanding boss. During the first two years of my marriage, when I had been away from Antwerp, he couldn't keep a secretary for any length of time!

My husband's job with one of the big maritime firms came to an end, and his efforts to leave for America increased. These efforts finally paid off, and on December 11, 1940, he left on the last train allowed by the German occupier to leave for Portugal via France.

This was definitely the point at which my life totally changed. I continued working for my father daily, leaving my apartment on the outskirts of town and covering the distance to his home and office on my bicycle in about twenty-five minutes, to start work promptly at 8:30 A.M. There were no fixed hours, officially, yet the workday terminated at 6 P.M., but I worked through to all hours, especially when there were court reports or balance sheets to go out.

Being my father's secretary also provided me with my only daily meal; I couldn't afford any other. In Belgium the main meal, dinner, is served at noon. My stepmother made sure that this daily meal was taken out of my pay, and she reduced my salary to less than half of what she would have had to pay anyone else for the job!

Food was rationed by the Germans, and we were issued monthly stamps. But as the months of occupation accumulated, the food-rationing tightened, and very often the items for which one had stamps were not to be found.

The black market was our savior. We were very glad it was available. What the black marketeers were selling was not withheld from the population; it was what the farmers managed to hide from the German requisitioners, thus depriving the enemy of its use and providing us with it—at a price, of course. But they ran great risks: if they were caught, the punishment was very severe.

My father was financially able to take advantage of these offerings, and our midday meal, although not as plentiful as before the war, was ample.

Part Two:
Belgian Resistance

1 Rumors about the organized resistance toward the Germans increased, and reports of executions of Resistance fighters also circulated. As hatred of the enemy grew, so did the underground movement. The desire to be part of this movement welled up in me.

One day in February, 1941, nine months after the German invasion of Belgium, I had a conversation with an acquaintance while coming home on the streetcar. We were on the platform, and our exchanges were, of course, in double talk when they had anything to do with the war or the army of occupation. But I had a funny feeling, like a sixth sense, that was telling me that this man was involved in the Resistance movement. This prompted me, as I was getting ready to get off the streetcar, to remark to him, "If I can help you in any way, let me know."

This was perfectly innocent. If I were overheard by enemy ears, I had many an explanation to justify this remark. It could have meant,

"If I can help you with one of my rations, when you are short . . ." or, "If your wife is not feeling well, give me a call, I'll come and help," etc.

The peculiar look he gave me in return to my remark gave me a feeling I had struck gold! Then one evening, less than two weeks later, the bell rang. This was always a reason for the adrenalin to shoot up. If you didn't expect anyone, a doorbell was quite often an unwanted "enemy" visitor, either for your arrest, or to search your dwelling.

My caller was the acquaintance from the streetcar. The moment he entered my apartment he said: "You have been checked; you can start working!"

Work started in earnest a few days later. My contact, Augustin, informed me that I was now a member of an intelligence network. I would start by typing reports to be sent on to England by means of the network's transmitter, located in Brussels. It was a father-and-son team who operated the transmitter out of their home.

My first reports seemed rather tedious material. At first glance, some of these pages appeared to be an unending listing of serial numbers. However, they were, in fact, most valuable information for the Allies in England. The numbers were the identification numbers of all trains and freight cars leaving Antwerp. The list recorded the contents of these cars, their departure times, and destinations. Antwerp had a tremendous network of marshaling yards, used to the fullest by the Nazi war machine.

Augustin visited me a few days later, accompanied by another member of the network. He was older than we were, had been a career Army man, and was the one with whom I would work most closely. His name was Hubin.

Hubin gave me my first active mission: I was to go and pick up the original reports myself that day. I was all excited, although admittedly apprehensive. Understandably so, for this was not just a matter of walking up to someone's desk or counter and asking for such and such a document!

The office I was to go to was situated near the port area of Antwerp. The neighborhood was the kind one didn't especially choose to walk through, but we were now a country occupied by a ruthless enemy, and these enemy troops and agents, civilian and uniformed, were everywhere.

The office where I was to contact our "source" was under the supervision of the Germans. I propped my bicycle in its parking spot, and, my heart beating at a fast pace, entered the office complex.

Contact was made, and there, at the big counter, the sheaf of papers was handed to me in plain view of uniformed Nazi soldiers. It was the first test of my control of my strong emotions. I told myself, "At all cost, look relaxed, matter of factly, no furtive looks, no hasty retreats!"

I walked out with my heart still pounding, but no outward expression betrayed me. In the eyes of those I passed by, I was a happy-go-lucky, carefree individual. But in reality I couldn't get far away from there fast enough. I jumped on my bike and pedaled at a good pace through the sinuous, cobblestone streets toward home.

Thus I was initiated into the *Groupe Général de Sabotage de Belgigue,* the General Sabotage Group of Belgium, or Group G as we called it.

I was still working for my father; therefore my Resistance activity was handled after office hours or during noon recess. I was determined never to confide anything of my Resistance activities to anyone, including my Father, although his patriotic sentiments were well known, and I remained true to that decision to the end.

However, strangely enough, one day my father asked me in double-talk fashion to get in contact with a friend's widow. This was very unusual, because there had never been such a rapport between my father and me.

Contact was made, and it turned out that the son of this friend was hiding from the Germans. He was a Belgian military fighter pilot who had been captured by the Germans and imprisoned. After several months he had escaped, and now wanted to rejoin the Allied forces in England. The young man was also in need of a hiding place in the meantime, for he was wanted by the Germans. I suggested he move into my apartment until we could get him on the way.

My father never inquired as to how, when, or if I had been able to do something. He surely guessed, but felt the necessity of not being a part of it. Ignorance was the best course of action.

The young airman was provided false identity papers, and a date for his departure was set. I was given the mission to escort him to Brussels, there to deliver him to another contact.

The electric train ride from Antwerp to Brussels took thirty-five minutes. One always risked being checked by the Gestapo upon departure or arrival or on the train itself during the journey. We were not stopped at embarkation, but halfway to Brussels two men, unmistakably Gestapo agents in civilian clothes, entered our compartment, scrutinizing the passengers. They demanded the papers of one man at the end of the compartment, then from another halfway toward us.

As they approached, I was afraid they might hear our heartbeats, but after merely staring us down they moved on to the next compartment. I assume our apparent innocent, carefree behavior saved us from certain arrest.

We had successfully completed the half-hour train trip from Antwerp to Brussels without incident, although not without anxiety, and now, breathing a little easier, we headed for the rendezvous, a little café in one of the suburbs of Brussels. I had been given very good directions, and found the café without any trouble. It was a small establishment in a quiet neighborhood. I seem to remember there weren't more than six tables, and a customer was seated at one of them. Was this my contact? It wasn't.

We ordered a beer, and by all outward appearances we were just two friends spending a few carefree minutes together. No one could have suspected our underlying tension.

Then the door opened and a middle-aged male civilian, rather tall and strongly built, walked in. He strolled leisurely to the table slightly ahead and to the right of ours, sat down, and ordered a libation. His eyes met mine. Both our stares were blank and impersonal, but after a few minutes the pre-arranged sequence of events began.

The instructions I had received about making contact and passing my young flyer on to the agent were as follows. The agent would be carrying the German magazine *Signal,* which was the size and type of the American *Life* magazine. This publication always had beautiful photographic coverage, and was full of war stories distorted to show the German armies in the field and on occupation duties. They were presented always in a rosy manner: heroic in the field, and benevolent toward the people under their heel.

When the agent was ready to take the airman with him, he would lift the magazine a certain way before leafing through it; then, getting up, he would accidentally drop it, pick it up, and deposit it back on the table while seeming to search his pockets for some imaginable item. Then, having supposedly found it, he would leave the establishment with the magazine tucked under his left arm.

As the pre-arranged sequence unfolded, the moment came for me to prepare my young flyer for action. I had, of course, not given any details of this arrangement to him, but when the agent headed for the door, I told the airman that he was to get up in a few seconds and walk out; that the gentleman he just saw leaving would be waiting for him in the street, and would take care of him.

The flyer, understandably, showed apprehension when he realized I would not accompany him. But such were the orders; I was not coming along on the next leg of his escape. He would have a danger-filled journey ahead. He and the agents who would escort him through Belgium, France, and Spain would hopefully reach their destination undetected, but the pitfalls were numerous. German agents —Gestapo, SS, GFP *(Geheime Feldpolizei)*—were everywhere. The escapees were provided with false identity papers which looked very authentic but did not always survive intense scrutiny. From Spain the escapees would be embarked clandestinely aboard a boat to England.

As I later learned, the airman made it safely to Spain, but there he was detected, arrested, and incarcerated.

2 In 1942 the German command in Belgium began a systematic harassment of the Jewish population. This harassment, which at first was surreptitious, intensified. All Jews were to wear an orange Star of David sewn on their garments. Their identity cards—which all Belgians, from age fourteen on, had to carry at all times under Belgian law—were stamped *Jude* (Jew) in big letters. Gentiles were forbidden to employ Jews. Jews who owned businesses were at the mercy of organized vandalism and destruction. The systematic annihilation of this segment of our population was in full swing. Antwerp, being a diamond center of the world, had consequently a big Jewish population.

The horrible "round-ups" were in process. The SS would stake out one neighborhood, and a moving van would be parked at a strategic point from which their agents would fan out in the neighborhood. Whomever they found at home was dragged out and forced into the van. So, for instance, a man and wife, being the only ones at home, would be taken; later, their child would return from school to find an empty house.

These vans had no ventilation and sometimes stood for hours, suffocating their occupants. These had been destined for one of

The Star of David was to be worn by all Jews, sewn on their garments above the heart.

Hitler's concentration camps in Germany, which for the majority meant extermination.

At one time in Antwerp, the SS had started rounding up all male Jews they could locate. The news spread like fire, and all those who could went in hiding. After a few days, the German command released the Belgian ones, saying they had been taken by mistake, that only foreign ones were targeted. This turned out to be a trick, to seduce those in hiding to come out of seclusion, reassured by this "official statement." Many did take the bait, unfortunately.

A few days after the release of this "official statement" one of the agents of my espionage network notified me that the SS was going to begin their second round-up twenty-four hours later, with the aim of capturing all the young Jewish men who had come out of hiding.

As I mentioned before, my husband's family was of Jewish origin. His younger brother lived with his parents. I rushed to their apartment and told him to get out. The parents were incredulous, repeating the assurance given by the German authorities, and felt their son was in no danger. I obviously couldn't reveal the source of my information, but pleaded with them not to let their son stay. He, without delay, heeded my advice and left. The same night, the SS knocked at their door and demanded that their son accompany them. In all truth, Mama told them he was not home and that she didn't know where he was!

Thus he was able to escape.

The increase in confinement rules, the abrogation of whatever liberties were still allowed, and the constant fear of a knock at the door caused my parents-in-law to accept shelter offered to them outside of Antwerp, and they, too, went into hiding.

The family who took them in were very simple working people living in very cramped conditions themselves. There were small children in the household, which didn't leave much quiet and calm, and increased the risk of detection. But the family's offer to take in and hide this Jewish couple was an act of great courage. If caught, they themselves faced certain arrest, deportation, or even execution!

Upon the departure of my parents-in-law, I, with the help of my girlfriend "Jimmy," proceeded one evening to try to save some of their belongings. If the German authorities discovered they had fled, they would immediately ransack the place.

The apartment building in which they had lived was located in a quiet residential neighborhood. Across from their building, however, was a small garage which had been requisitioned by the German Army. Luckily, the Germans generally closed shop after dark, but one never knew if and where there was a guard.

My girlfriend and I took the elevator to the third floor. I had been given the key to the apartment. We entered apprehensively, and tiptoed in; we didn't want our presence broadcast through the building. We took a large wicker laundry basket and started collecting clothing and a variety of items we didn't want to fall into the hands of the enemy.

We moved with alacrity and as quietly as possible, but in the midst of our mission we suddenly perceived some movement outside the door. We stood frozen, practically holding our breath. The dreaded knock on the door came. We were going to be caught red-handed helping a Jewish family. Arrest on the spot was certain, deportation or execution could follow.

I went to the front door and opened it. What a relief! There stood the neighbor from the floor below, who, knowing the owners were gone and having detected a presence, was investigating.

She, in turn, was pleased to realize what our mission was.

Jimmy lived about three blocks away and we took the Jewish couple's belongings to her house. Luckily, the night was a pitch-black, moonless one. Jimmy lived with her mother and niece. The mother, whom I affectionately called "Bobonne," had been a widow for most of her life. She owned and lived in the three-story house, and it was a three-woman household. It was very brave on their part to have accepted to keep in storage whatever belongings of the Jewish couple—really strangers to them—with which I was burdening them.

Jimmy and I emptied our big wicker basket at Bobonne's and returned to the apartment for a second load. Half an hour later on the ten-minute return trip, as we rounded the corner of the second block and had gone about fifty feet, Jimmy ran into a big electric box which stood on the sidewalk. We knew very well of the existence of this box, but I guess our haste on this risky mission, combined with the pitch-dark, moonless night, caused this hard encounter. Poor Jimmy hit the box full force, causing a very painful swelling in her forehead. Incredibly, this accident, despite the physical pain, caused us to break out in one of those irrepressible laughing spells, breaking the tension we had been working under.

Arriving home with our second load and the visible result of Jimmy's encounter with the electric box, we were faced with Bobonne's refusal to let her daughter return to the apartment for another load. However, she very generously stated she was willing to accept another load, if I wanted to go back to the apartment one more time alone. And I did.

I couldn't blame Bobonne for her stand. They were already running a big risk by agreeing to store the belongings in their home. Once again: if found out, they faced imprisonment and whatever additional possible sentence.

All these efforts turned out to be for naught. The parents-in-law left their hiding place after a few weeks and returned to their apartment in Antwerp.

With the ever-increasing SS program of arrest and extermination of the Jewish population, this couple didn't escape, and the day came when they were taken away and shipped to a camp in Malines—a small town about halfway between Antwerp and Brussels. The camp was a holding camp where prisoners were kept until being shipped to a German concentration camp.

There was nothing one could do for them once they were incarcerated there, except to send packages of food and basic needs, but, there was never any certainty that the prisoners would receive any of it.

One day I decided to deliver a package myself. This was not exactly a daily occurrence, and I was taking a big risk, but felt it was my duty. The big gate loomed forbiddingly ahead. I rang. It seemed ages before the big door opened. A surprised guard inquired about my business, and I showed him the package. I was told in no uncertain terms that packages were not to be delivered to prisoners, but I stood my ground. This was perhaps the first time I experienced what seemed to be a German military trait: when you stood up to them, they respected you the more for it.

The guard seemed to hesitate, then told me: *Ein Moment* (just a moment), and slammed the big door shut. A few minutes later the door opened again and there stood an officer holding a German shepherd on a short leash. Despite my fear of dogs, I tried to appear calm and collected. I repeated my request to deliver my parcel. After an exchange of several requests and denials, the officer finally gave in and accepted the package.

As was to be feared, however, those for whom the package was intended never received it; and again as feared, the reports later told that all parcels were checked by the SS, who removed whatever they could use.

It was also reported that at the camp in Malines dogs—those German shepherds—were used to torture the prisoners. The dogs were sicked on the prisoners at the slightest whim of the jailers. It might be as a general punishment, or, when the prisoners were herded back inside, those not moving fast enough, or physically handicapped, were attacked by the viciously trained dogs.

3 Our espionage network had been gathering and broadcasting for about one and a half years when disaster struck.

As mentioned earlier, the transmitter was located in Brussels, in a private residence in care of a father-and-son operation. One day the Gestapo arrived and forced their way inside. The son was able to escape, but his father was killed.

The son immediately notified the sector chiefs of this disaster, and, of course, the instant order to all agents was to "lie low." All our activities stopped.

The frustration caused by this stoppage in our activity was tremendous. Apprehension was certainly lurking in the background, even if one didn't want to admit it to oneself. But being completely in the dark as to the origin of the raid on our transmitter location was the main cause of our anguish.

Had we been betrayed? If so, by whom? A "collaborator," a friend of the German occupation forces? Was it an "inside" job? Did we have an informer among our agents? Whatever the cause, it became obvious that the Nazis were on our trail. One after the other, several of our agents were arrested.

We could feel the net tightening around us. Augustin, my first contact with the Resistance, the one who enrolled me in the network, was by all indications next in line for arrest. He spotted it immediately when the surveillance began, and no time was lost in getting him out.

Augustin's journey would be a long and hazardous one. There were two borders to cross: from Belgium into France, then France into Spain, and there was the constant risk of being stopped, questioned as to his activity or reason for being in such a spot, and having his false identity papers scrutinized. He made it safely into France; however, halfway through the country on his way to the Spanish border, he was ambushed and murdered.

Since the order had come from England to "lie low," I had had very little contact with Hubin, the Belgian military career man. We had to avoid contact, in view of the Germans' systematic rounding-up of our agents. We had escaped so far.

The attitude of the occupier toward the Belgian population was becoming more hostile and repressive. Gone was the obvious order from the high command to the Nazi troops to try to make friends with the occupied population. Radios were to be turned in in order to prevent us from listening to the BBC. Curfews were imposed more and more frequently, generally as a result of some act of aggression or revolt against the German forces, or following some act of sabotage against them. This increased "prisoner" status of the Belgian citizens created more and more anti-German feelings and activity.

The stirrings of opposition by the citizens in general had been present since the first day of occupation, and grew in intensity and imagination. At first their opposition amounted to little more than a show of insolence toward the occupier. But just as the constant buzzing of an insect around one's head begins as an annoyance, it leads to exterminating the culprit. So did the constant barbs toward the occupier bring stronger and stronger retaliations. These retaliations, in turn, aroused the ire of the Belgians, and the Resistance movements grew.

It was 1941, July 21, Belgian National Day. No Belgian flags were, of course, allowed to be displayed, so I decided to dress up in the Belgian National colors: a black skirt, red blouse, and yellow belt. My girlfriend also put the three colors on display, and off we went to the city's main shopping area.

It was a delight to acknowledge the reaction of the population! People pressed their hands in a congratulatory gesture; others applauded loudly; others called out "Bravo!" We had a ball. Luckily, our outing ended without trouble.

Our activities exposed us, of course, to the constant threat of arrest. The following incident illustrates this point.

At the conclusion of a meeting of our cell of the espionage network, a British agent who was present asked me to take his gun back with me and keep it until the next meeting. Possession of a firearm—and more so carrying one—was punishable by execution.

A few weeks later we had another meeting with the British agent, and I was instructed to bring his gun. I debated on the safest way to carry the weapon. In my big handbag? In a tote bag, covered with miscellaneous items? Which one would be the safest in case I were stopped and searched for whatever reason?

I discarded both of these ideas, and boldly decided to simply slip the gun in the right side-pocket of my jacket. Oversized pockets were in vogue, so the gun slipped in easily and showed no bulge. Off I went on my bicycle, toward our meeting place.

When I arrived at one of the big intersections, all traffic was stopped and a Gestapo search exercise was in progress. Ahead of me was a truck; the Gestapo checked the driver's papers, checked the truck, then walked toward me.

I was standing straddling my bicycle, my right foot on the sidewalk. I gave the agent a big smile. He looked me over, and inquisitively in a harsh tone barked: *"Haben Sie keine Tasche?"* (Don't you have a handbag?) In a carefree tone, smiling, I replied: *"Nein, Nichts!"* (No, Nothing!) He hesitated for a moment, then said: *"Gut, gehen Sie!"* (All right, go.) He had been standing less than two feet from me; less than two feet from my pocket containing the firearm!

Once again, luck had been with me!

4 Hubin paid me a visit a couple of months after the temporary shut-down of the espionage network. As soon as he entered my apartment he said, "Would you like to start working again?" I couldn't believe my ears, and enthusiastically responded: "Of course!"

"Ah! but this will be another type of work," he said.

"Well, tell me quickly, what does it consist of?" I asked.

"Sabotage" was the response!

Hubin started briefing me on some of the particulars. We would, at present, have to provide our own devices; the targets, at this point, would be German communication centers.

And work started in earnest. My dining/living room became a laboratory whenever we put together incendiary bombs. The containers resembled the milk cartons, like those sold in United States markets. We had to combine several ingredients. Not being a chemist, I can't remember what they were; however, I remember clearly that one was sugar. Why do I remember this detail? Because sugar was one of the rationed food items!

Then there were the little glass tubes—like aspirin vials—to be filled with sulfuric acid and corked. The cork had to be pierced beforehand with a red-hot knitting needle. This provided a rather strong odor that permeated the apartment. After the vial of sulfuric acid was thus closed up with the cork, a certain type of paper, folded in a certain way, was inserted into the hole.

The vial was the wick for the fire bomb. When the saboteur got to his target, he would plant the carton, then take the vial and turn it upside down into the carton; the sulfuric acid would slowly saturate the folded paper in the orifice, then drip into the mixture and cause ignition. This procedure gave the saboteur time to leave the premises and be out of danger of detection.

This brings to mind one day when Hubin and I were seated at my big dining room table and had already filled six of the cartons with the prescribed mixture. I had lined them up on the covered keyboard of my upright piano, which stood against the wall facing one end of the table. On top of the piano stood the big bottle of sulfuric acid. Suddenly, Hubin stared in a frozen expression and, pointing to the piano, whispered: "Yvonne . . . Mitsy!" Mitsy was my black cat. There she was, on top of the piano, slinking around the bottle of acid, ready to topple it over onto the six incendiary bombs below! No need to emphasize the sigh of relief when I was able to retrieve her gently, and thus avoid a catastrophe of enormous proportions!

Another sabotage instrument, a very effective contraption, was used to destroy the tires on the German vehicles. Cars and trucks were very important targets, for the Germans were feeling the pinch of a very big shortage of rubber.

These contraptions were marvelously conceived, and each was handmade by one of our men. They came in two or three sizes; the biggest ones destined for heavier types of vehicles. They consisted of a V-shaped base affixed to an upright hollow prong. The device was slipped under the wheel of a vehicle, and when the vehicle started the prong embedded itself in the tire; the base broke off, and the prong allowed the air to escape, and at each turn of the wheel it shredded the tire. It was a very effective destructive device!

I was one of those assigned to place these devices. Slipping them under the wheels of parked German vehicles was a very risky task. There were hundreds of eyes all around, if not right there on the street, then peering from windows above. A figure bending over close to a military vehicle and crouching there long enough to place a device was quite conspicuous. I did it many times, however, and was undetected; but, oh my! the adrenalin! Did it flow fast every time!

5 The clandestine press grew. From simple mimeographed sheets passed from patriot to patriot, some publications developed into professional periodicals. *La Libre Belgigue* was one of those. Tabloid-size, with a bold banner on top, it was quite informative, and by its "clandestinity" alone, quite morale-boosting. Another good journal was *La Voix des Belges.*

Some of the mimeographed material was directed, on the other hand, to the occupation forces—to the enemy. Here the purpose was to sap their morale by giving them the real news about the war: figures about their losses in manpower, and about the tremendous destruction inflicted by the Allied bombings of the home front. The German command, the German radio, and German press all covered up those facts.

A friend of mine who was active in the clandestine press asked me if I would help distribute some of these mimeographed publications. They were to be slipped into the letterboxes of apartment buildings requisitioned and occupied by German military personnel.

The streets of Antwerp were quite deserted at night, except for the Germans. The gray, green, and black uniforms of the enemy were visible at all hours. The civilians were very sparse, except right on the main thoroughfare in the center of town, and these "civil-

N° 17   15 AOUT 1941

LA LIBRE BELGIQUE

NOUVELLE SÉRIE DE GUERRE
FONDÉE LE 15 AOUT 1940

RÉDACTION ET ADMINISTRATION : OBERFELDKOMMANDANTUR. I, PLACE DU TRONE. BRUXELLES

EDITEUR RESPONSABLE : PETER PAN, JARDIN D'EGMONT, BRUXELLES

J'ai lot dans nos destinées. Un pays qui se défend s'impose au respect de tous. Ce pays ne périt pas ! Dieu nous aura avec nous dans cette cause juste.
ALBERT, Roi des Belges

Acceptons provisoirement les sacrifices qui nous sont imposés et attendons patiemment l'heure de la réparation.
A. MAX.

Envers les personnes qui détiennent par la force militaire notre pays, ayons les égards que commande l'intérêt général. Respectons les règlements qu'elles nous imposent aussi longtemps qu'ils ne portent atteinte ni à la liberté ni à nos convictions chrétiennes, ni à notre dignité patriotique.
Monseigneur MERCIER.

Entre le sacrifice et le déshonneur, le Belge de 1940 n'hésite pas plus que celui de 1914. L'exile sera dure, mais son ne peut douter du succès final. La cause de la Belgique est pure. Avec l'aide de Dieu, elle triomphera.
LEOPOLD.

Quelle que soit la durée de l'épreuve à subir, tous les Belges doivent avoir pour mot d'ordre " Tous le Roi, tout ou sers ».
F.-J. VAN DE MEULEBROEK.

Sans doute celui accessoire de reconnaître le pouvoir écrasant comme un souverain de fait et de lui obéir dans dans les limites des conventions internationales mais la Patrie Belgique n'existe et tous les enfants lui doivent fidélité et dévoûment.
Monseigneur VAN ROEY.

Double Anniversaire

Il y a un an que deux citoyens belges, animés des mêmes sentiments du plus pur patriotisme, estimaient qu'ils avaient le devoir de reprendre la lourde tâche de leurs aînés et de faire reparaître cette « Libre Belgique » de 1914-1918 qui avait tant fait pour soutenir le moral des Belges pendant les sombres et douloureuses années de l'occupation.

Avec leurs seuls moyens financiers (et ils étaient modestes) mais avec une inépuisable énergie ils mirent sur pied ce petit journal qui n'a fait que grandir.

Mais peut-être n'eussent-ils jamais réussi d'une façon aussi éclatante s'ils n'avaient eu la bonne fortune de trouver et de réunir autour d'eux des collaborateurs intelligents et dévoués auxquels ils éprouvent le besoin d'adresser leurs remerciements après 12 mois d'efforts tenaces et parfois pénibles. A nos rédacteurs, à nos prospecteurs, à nos porteurs, à notre imprimeur, à tous nous disons cordialement « MERCI », et nous leur demandons de redoubler d'efforts pour que notre journal atteigne, grâce à eux, une diffusion plus grande encore.

Au seuil de cette seconde année nous croyons avoir atteint le but que nous nous étions fixés. nous croyons, dans nos informations, être restés fidèles à la Constitution de notre Pays et avoir respecté son article 18 relatif à la liberté de la Presse. Nous croyons aussi nous être approché des directives données à tous les Belges par la lettre pastorale de Monseigneur Van Roey le 10 février 1941 :

« La charité a aussi en ce moment un beau rôle moral à remplir. Il existe tant de foyers visités par l'adversité, ou en deuil d'un père ou d'un fils tombé à la guerre, ou anxieux au sujet d'un prisonnier impatiemment attendu. D'autres gens se laissent aller au découragement par ignorance du cours véritable des événements ou par suite de nouvelles déformées et tendancieuses. Rien de plus méritoire que de consoler les affligés, de réconforter les faibles, de combattre le pessimisme et de faire renaître dans les cœurs la confiance ».

Nous sommes fiers d'avoir pu, grâce au soutien que chacun de nos lecteurs nous a apporté, augmenter la diffusion de notre journal à un point tel, que son tirage dépasse largement celui de son aîné de 1914-1918.

Il faut en effet, que chacun sache que « La Libre Belgique » n'est soutenue par aucun groupement et que sa raison d'être n'a qu'un but : maintenir le moral de notre population jusqu'au jour où, entouré des ailes de la victoire anglaise, condition première au recouvrement de notre indépendance et de nos libertés, elle pourra crier avec nous : « Vive le Roi ! » « Vive la Belgique ! ».

Si le 15 août est le jour anniversaire de notre journal, le hasard veut que, depuis un an aussi notre ennemi n° 1 devrait se promener dans les rues de la « CITY ».

Après la défaite française le Führer avait en effet annoncé aux quatre coins du monde, que ses hordes défileraient à Londres le 15 août suivant; son astrologue et ses pythonisses le lui avaient affirmé ! Fort de ses prédictions il lança ses premières attaques aériennes d'envergure sur la Grande Bretagne, elles furent toutes repoussées. Le mois d'août passa... Au mois de septembre nouvelle attaque, nouveau désastre, cette fois dans l'air et sur mer. Depuis lors, les boches piétinent rageusement devant les 40 km. d'eau qui les séparent de ce qu'ils croyaient une proie facile.

Le manque de matières premières les a obligés à attaquer l'U.R.S.S. Liée par une amitié éternelle et conformément au pacte existant celle-ci invita les guerriers de la Grande Allemagne à passer leurs quartiers d'hiver sur son territoire. Pendant ce temps la R.A.F. distribue chaque jour à leur industrie TOUS LES METAUX QUI LUI MANQUENT. Comme on le voit, le Führer et son peuple sont comblés, l'U.R.S.S. et la R.A.F. les protègent ! La Victoire est en marche...

Août 1941 — Scandale à Berlin :
Le Führer est en retard d'un an sur le programme que lui avaient assigné les signaleurs de routes.

SCIPION L'AFRICAIN et PETER PAN

N° 11   PRIX DU NUMÉRO : 1 FRANC   22 MARS 1942

BATTUS PARFOIS, ABATTUS JAMAIS

REGARDS SUR DEMAIN

La question des Ministres

Donc, nous avons dit l'autre fois que nous voulions l'ordre dans l'État de demain: chacun à sa place et demeurant dans la sphère des attributions : un pouvoir Exécutif, qui soit maître et gouverne et une assemblée nationale, qui contrôle.

Dans le domaine de l'Exécutif nous voudrions, aujourd'hui, dire quelques mots des Ministres.

⁂

Pour rappeler d'abord que, au sein du gouvernement, ils ne sont pas les « représentants d'un parti », mais les Ministres du Roi.

Dans la vie courante, que ce soit dans une entreprise industrielle ou familiale, c'est le chef de l'entreprise qui choisit ses collaborateurs. Les Ministres du Roi doivent être nommés par le Roi: nous estimons que ce doit être plus littéralement vrai encore pour le Premier Ministre, qui doit jouir de toute la confiance du Souverain.

Dans notre esprit, le Premier Ministre devrait avoir une prééminence réelle et reconnue sur ses collègues, et diriger effectivement la politique du pays. Ce devrait être son rôle, à l'exclusion de la gestion d'un Département quelconque.

⁂

Les Ministres sont membres du conseil de la Couronne. A ce titre, ils servent le chef de l'État et l'État lui-même, c'est-à-dire la collectivité nationale. C'est pourquoi on ne [...]

On a souvent agité le problème de la responsabilité ministérielle. Il ne se pose vraiment que lorsque, sous la pression de la politicaille, des hommes douteux accèdent à des fonctions pour lesquelles ils ne sont pas indiqués. Un homme d'État intègre, consciencieux, averti et prudent n'a pas besoin d'une loi réglant la responsabilité des Ministres pour savoir où est son devoir. L'accomplir, et s'arrêter d'instinct devant l'équivoque ou le risque. Le choix des Ministres est avant tout un problème de moralité. N'ayons pas peur de ce mot, qui ne fait ricaner que ceux qui font fi de la chose.

On peut se demander si, avant le 10 mai, les Ministres ont toujours tous été des modèles à cet égard; et si tous ne l'ont pas été, n'est-ce pas parce que la politique s'est fourrée dans certaines nominations ? Que la leçon porte ses fruits.

⁂

Faut-il cinq Ministres, ou dix, ou quinze ? On peut se battre à ce sujet. Leur nombre n'a de réelle importance qu'en ce qui concerne les réunions du conseil des Ministres. Si ce conseil devient, par son ampleur, un petit parlement, il en aura tous les vices et toutes les lenteurs. Quel que soit le nombre des Ministres, il n'en faudrait que quelques-uns qui constituent le « Cabinet » proprement dit: il faudrait que ce Cabinet traitât seul, sous la présidence du Premier Ministre, tous les grands problèmes de l'État. Pareille réforme serait utilement introduite dans le [...]

---

ians" were not necessarily some brave Belgians venturing out before curfew; they could well have been one of the German SS, the *Geheime Feldpolizei* (Secret Field Police), or the Gestapo.

Stopping at all the German-occupied buildings and slipping printed matter into all the letterboxes would be no child's play. The danger of detection lurked at each step, and with it the inevitable arrest, interrogation, torture, deportation, or even execution.

Many Belgians involved in either the printing or distribution of the clandestine press were caught. Lady Luck continued to be on my side, however.

There were also leaflet drop missions by the Allied air forces. These leaflets were excellent propaganda instruments, carrying their messages on the winds far and wide. They served a good purpose, and supplemented our efforts. Victor, our chief saboteur, brought me one of them he had picked up as it floated to earth. It was a dilly, and was bound to impress the Germans stationed here. It depicted a battlefield on the Russian front, strewn with masses of dead German soldiers sprawled across the snow-covered ground. Hitler stood amidst them, smiling, and saying: *"Ich fühle mich so frisch. Es kommt der Frühling."* (I feel so 'fresh.' Spring is coming.) On the back was a message to "The soldiers of the Wehrmacht," attacking the cause for which they were fighting. The pamphlet also quoted some of the ravings of Hitler and Göring about the power and invincibility of the German Luftwaffe. Opposite this, it showed the true situation, and the superiority of the Allies.

Hitler's treacherous attack on Russia—his supposed ally—on June 22, 1941, seemed incredible, but it brought a resurgence of hope to us in the opposition; his opening a second front would inevitably sap his manpower.

Russian prisoners suddenly appeared in my neighborhood. The first time I saw them, one early morning as I was getting ready to leave for the office, I heard an unusual "marching" sound approaching, so I opened one of my big windows and leaned outside.

My apartment was situated on the outskirts of town in a lovely residential area adjacent to three huge beautiful parks. The occupation forces obviously appreciated the living conditions there, and had requisitioned several of the apartment buildings; the coming and going of military personnel was constant on our avenue.

Coming toward my end of the street was a group of men, marching in four columns five men deep, dejected, heads bent down, dressed shabbily, under the command of a German *Feldwebel* (sergeant), who marched on the sidewalk alongside them.

They passed directly under my window, then at the corner, fifty feet further down, turned into a cross-street. The thought came to

"Ich fühle mich so frisch.
Es kommt der Frühling."

(ADOLF HITLER, 24. 2. 41.)

AN DIE SOLDATEN DER DEUTSCHEN WEHRMACHT!

"KEIN deutscher Soldat kann sagen, dass er für eine gerechte Sache kämpfe. Er muss sehen, dass man ihn· zwingt, Krieg zu führen, um andere Völker auszurauben und zu unterdrücken."

„ Die Stärke der Roten Armee liegt vor allem· in der Tatsache, dass sie keinen Rassenhass gegen andere Völker, auch nicht gegen das deutsche Volk, kennt. Die Rote Armee ist im Geiste der Gleichberechtigung aller Völker und Rassen erzogen worden und durch die Achtung vor den Rechten anderer Nationen gross geworden."

„ Manchmal faselt die ausländische Presse davon, dass das Sowjetvolk die Deutschen als Deutsche hasse, dass die Rote Armee deutsche Soldaten nur deshalb töte, weil Deutsche sind, aus Hass gegen das ganze deutsche Volk; und dass deshalb die Rote Armee keine Gefangene mache. Das ist eine dumme Lüge und eine bösartige Verleumdung der Roten Armee."

„ Das Ziel der Roten Armee ist die Vertreibung der deutschen faschistischen Eindringlinge aus unserem Land. Es ist durchaus wahrscheinlich, dass der Befreiungskrieg der Sowjet-Union entweder zur Vernichtung oder zur Vertreibung der Hitlerklique führen wird. Wir werden einen solchen Ausgang nur willkommen heissen. Die Hitlerklique darf nicht mit dem deutschen Volk verwechselt werden. Die Geschichte lehrt, dass die Hitlers kommen und gehen, aber das deutsche Volk und der deutsche Staat bleiben."

Diese Worte sagte Stalin am 23. Februar 1942, dem 24. Jahrestag der Gründung der Roten Armee.

Damit hat sich Stalin noch einmal für das Prinzip eines gerechten Friedens ausgesprochen, das er schon in seiner Rede am 2. Juli 1942 betont hat; ein Prinzip, das auch in der Roosevelt-Churchill-Erklärung enthalten ist:

„ Grossbritannien und die Vereinigten Staaten von Amerika anerkennen für jedes Volk das Recht, die Regierungsform zu wählen, unter der es leben will."

Churchill, Stalin und Roosevelt haben dieses Prinzip des gerechten Friedens natürlich nicht aus reinem Idealismus verkündet. Im Interesse ihrer eigenen Völker sind sie entschlossen, Deutschland gegenüber nicht die Methoden des Rassenhasses und der wirtschaftlichen Ausbeutung anzuwenden, die Hitlerdeutschland gegen andere Völker benutzt.

DEUTSCHER SOLDAT! Du kämpfst für den Mann und das System, die allein den Weg versperren zu

EINEM GERECHTEN FRIEDEN!

G.12

43

"Von der Maas bis an die Memel..."

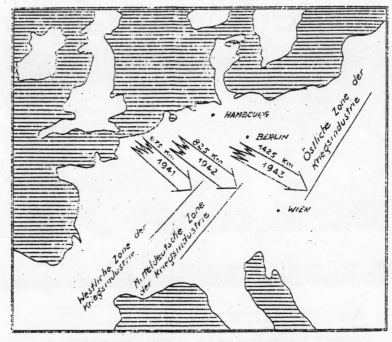

"Nach Ostland wollen wir reiten"..... erinnert Ihr Euch ? Der <u>Drank</u>
<u>nach Osten</u> ist wieder auf der Tagesordnung. Die deutsche Kriegsin-
dustrie wandert von Westdeutschland dem zukünftigen Niemandsland
des Luftkrieges nach Osten. Mit Sack und Pack und Werkstätten und
Fabriken ziehen Sie nach Prag, Wien und Warschau. Und hinter Ihnen
drängt die R.A.F. nach. Die neuen britischen Bomben haben eine
fünfmal stärkere Sprengkraft als alle früheren; und die riesigen
neuen britischen und amerikanischen Bombenflugzeuge wie der "Short
Stirling" und der "American Consolidated Liberator" könnten wenn
nötig, zweimal von England nach Warschau und zurück fliegen, ohne
zu tanken. Erinnert Euch, was Euch Göring am 9. August 1939 ver-
sprochen hat: "Wir werden das Ruhrgebiet auch nicht einer einzigen
Bombe feindlicher Flieger aussetzen!"
Und vergesst nicht, was Hitler am März 1941 gesagt hat:

" Ich habe jede Möglichkeit von vornherein einkalkuliert. "
=================

Ouvriers français
en Allemagne !
RAF
V
Ceci est le symbole de
votre libération.
Employez-le !!!

Lavoratori Italiani
in Germania!
RAF
V
Questo è il simbolo
della vostra liberazione
Usatelo !!!

Nederlandsche Arbeiders
in Duitschland !
RAF
V
Dit is het teeken van
Uw bevrijding
Gebruikt het !!!

Robotnicy Polscy
w Niemczech !
RAF
V
Ota symbol waszego
wyzwolenia Pamietajcie
o tem !!!

Uberall im besetzten Westen, in Frankreich, Holland und
Belgien findet man diese Buchstaben auf Wänden, Türen und
Bürgersteigen von unbekannten Händen mit Kreide hundert-
tausendfach angeschrieben. Jedes Kind in diesen drei
Ländern weiss, was die Buchstaben bedeuten.
RAF heisst Royal Air Force (Britische Luftwaffe). Sie
ist der Freund der unterdrückten und ausgebeuteten Völker
und der Bote der Hoffnung und der Ermutigung. Sie ist es
aber auch, die die deutschen Kasernen, Flugplätze, Schiffe,
Werften, Munitions und Öllager mitten in den besetzten
Ländern in Trümmer legt.
V heisst dreierlei: Für die Franzosen und Wallonen bedeutet es VICTOIRE (Sieg) und VENGEANCE (Vergeltung), für
die Holländer und Flamen bedeutet es VRIJHEID (Freiheit).
Aber für alle diese Völker hat es denselben Sinn: die
entgültige Erledigung Hitlers und des Dritten Reichs.
Diese Völker wissen gut, dass ihre Freunde, die RAF,
dank der vereinigten Kräfte Englands und Amerikas, den
Tag des Sieges, der Vergeltung und der Befreiung immer
näher bringen!

Es kommt der Tag !

==========

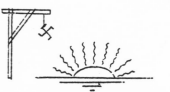

45

Die R.A.F. wirft jetzt in einer Nacht
1 bis 2 Millionen
Kilogramm Bomben

Bei ihrem schwersten Angriff auf London (10. Mai 1941) warf die Luftwaffe 450 000 Kilogramm Bomben. ..
Bei ihren „Grossangriffen" auf London im Frühling 1943 warf die Luftwaffe niemals mehr als 6 000 Kilogramm Bomben in einer Nacht.

Bis zum 25. Mai 1943 hat die R.A.F. die ersten
100 000 t Bomben
auf Deutschland abgeworfen

„Die nächsten 100 000 t werden noch wirksamer sein und werden rascher kommen."
Air Marshal Harris, 30. Mai 1943

G. 36

me that they were headed for a garage the Germans had taken over as a workshop. This and the appearance of the men let me immediately guess they were prisoners of the Germans. This was confirmed to me a short time later, and I learned also that they were Russian.

I felt a desperate need to do something for those poor devils who had fallen into the hands of our common enemy. The following morning I placed a portable record player on the wide marble sill inside my window, and as I heard the prisoners approach I started playing a record. I didn't have any Russian recordings, so I played Hungarian music, the rhythm of which was similar to their native music, and would, I was sure, stir them up, and combat their depression.

As they approached, one of the heads straightened up, and looked around, obviously in search of the origin of this music. A second head looked up, and a third. They suddenly spotted my window, and big smiles showed on their faces. One of the men brought both his hands in front of him and pressed them together in a warm gesture of thanks.

From that day on, I repeated the musical interlude each morning, and the spirits of the prisoners began to change. They marched erect, their smiling faces visible proof of the balm provided to their souls by the music.

Through a Belgian civilian working in the requisitioned garage, I was also able to smuggle some tidbits of food to them, which they could easily munch there, or take back to their detention quarters.

One day, however, I made a stupid mistake.

I had received, a few days before, a package of Belgian chocolate. An old-time friend of my father's had come to visit, especially to deliver to me this precious item. It was worth its weight in gold; no chocolate had been available since the occupation. He obviously had taken it out of his own hidden treasure chest!

You have to have experienced deprivation to realize how much a simple gift can mean.

Now I decided on another way to help the prisoners. That morning, as soon as I detected the approach of the marching platoon of prisoners, I ran down the two flights of stairs and walked down the avenue toward the approaching Feldwebel. I bluntly asked him if it would be possible to give his prisoners a few sweets. The Feldwebel was quite taken aback by my straightforward question, and also by what he obviously considered incredible boldness.

His answer, as expected, was a clear *Nein! "Nein, das ist ganz verboten"* (No, that is totally forbidden) was his retort, harsh and definitive.

I let a couple of days pass, then confronted the Feldwebel again with the same request. I added this time the question, "How would you feel if you were a prisoner?" He hesitated, then said: All right but he would come and get it, and he would give it to the men. He said he would come to pick it up that evening.

In the evening, Hubin, the chief of materiel of sabotage Group G, was in my apartment, going over some details. He knew I was expecting the Feldwebel to pick up my little package, and I had cut several of the chocolate bars into bite-size pieces for the prisoners to share. But when I opened the front door, there stood the Feldwebel, all dressed up in a clean uniform and polished boots, and ready to walk in—and visit!

I stood in the doorway, barring his entrance, and handed him the package for the prisoners. He expressed his astonishment at not being invited in, and left obviously piqued.

When I returned upstairs Hubin and I laughed at the discomfiture of the German, and at the irony of it all. If he only knew what was going on here daily against his own kind, in this very apartment!

Unfortunately, the last laugh was on me. The Russian prisoners had by now found a way to send me little scraps of paper with notes in German thanking me for the little gifts. But after I gave the last little package to their jailer for delivery to them, I received not the slightest sign of acknowledgment, neither by hand gesture as they walked by, nor by one of their delightful messages. I started wondering. Finally I asked them about it in one of my smuggled notes, and received a reply which stated: *"Der Teufel hat der schokolade gegessen."* (The devil has eaten the chocolate.) Thus, the Feldwebel got the last laugh; he never delivered the precious chocolate, but ate it himself!

What else should I have expected?

6   The activities of Group G grew quickly in scope due to the advent of the marvelous air-drops. Instead of our painstakingly homemade sabotage devices, there now came from England magnificent twenty-five and fifty-pound metal drums filled with all sorts of material to be used for sabotage: PE2, the putty-like substance used for our explosive charges; fuse cord; delay pencils; Sten guns; ammunition; and more. They came to depots in Brussels and Malines; Malines is about halfway between Brussels and Antwerp, twelve miles south of Antwerp.

The sabotage missions increased. Our main targets were still railroads, marshaling yards, and communication centers.

My apartment had become the headquarters for northern Belgium, and the sector chiefs would meet there to discuss strategy and missions. One of these meetings caused me a moment of alarm the following day.

On the ground floor lived a divorced man and his seven- or eight-year-old daughter. He was what I would call a rather cowardly type. At the slightest anti-aircraft activity he would bundle up his daughter and make her hole-up in the cellar—a cellar which would hardly qualify as a bomb shelter. I said many times I felt much safer in my top-floor apartment than in that cellar, which I feared would collapse under the weight of the entire building if we were ever to be hit. At least I could ride down!

That morning, after the meeting of the sector chiefs, I had just completed assembling the necessary materials for two or three sabotage missions which had been planned at a meeting the previous evening. The stick of explosives, the necessary lengths of cord, capsules, delay pencils, etc., were tightly packed in one of my zipper bags, which I generally hung on the handlebars of my bicycle or strapped on the rear luggage rack. The bag stood on my kitchen table. As I grabbed it and my jacket, there was a knock at the door. It was the neighbor. He walked in and immediately began admonishing me about the type of people I was entertaining.

I had to make an effort not to show amusement, and pretended to be offended by his remark. I told him my life was none of his business. "Are you paying my rent?" I asked. His answer being negative, I was, I repeated, seeing whom I wanted and when I wanted!

His visit was no surprise to me. The night before, when the men arrived, I was sure he was peeking from behind his curtains as he listened to the garden gate opening, and the steps coming toward the front door. He obviously couldn't resist taking a closer look when the sector chief from Limburg rang the bell, and as I came down and opened the front door, the neighbor came out of his apartment. The sector chief presented quite an impressive appearance. He was rather tall and slim, with jet-black hair that he greased down solidly. He had a dark complexion, with a pronounced five-o'clock shadow no matter how closely shaven he might be. He dressed in black, including a leather jacket and black boots, an outfit very helpful during his nighttime sabotage missions: he could easily pass for a German SS at a distance, and was inconspicuous to the occupier.

I admit, the man was certainly not the type of friend with whom I had been used to associating. But these were different times, and my activities were different. This was war, and I was engaged in sabotage against the enemy, and these men were my associates in our fight for the freedom of Belgium. So my neighbor's nosy interference was amusing to me, but I didn't let on that I had expected some reaction from him.

What worried me, however, was his behavior in the few seconds that followed.

I tried to get him out of my apartment, and get on my way to deliver my explosives. I told him I was in a hurry; would he excuse me, I had to leave. But instead of turning toward the door, he stepped into the kitchen, and extended his arm to touch my zipper bag. I stopped his gesture in mid-air by blurting out a mocking remonstrance at his obvious nosiness. He smiled sheepishly and left. But both incidents—checking on my visitors, and now his interest in the contents of my bag—raised the red flag of forewarning.

I took off on my bicycle; I had a long ride ahead—at least forty-five minutes. I had to meet some men on the outer edge of the suburbs on the opposite side of town. Main streets and boulevards had to be avoided for fear of being caught in a search exercise, so I took off along the moats around the caserne and followed the outer by ways.

After a few miles, something didn't seem right in the flow of bicycle traffic; there seemed to be an unusual haste in those going in the opposite direction.. Many were carrying jute sacks strapped on their luggage racks, filled with smuggled potatoes or grain. I hailed a cyclist coming toward me and asked if everything was okay ahead; it wasn't! "Checkpoint ahead!" he yelled. If I hadn't asked I would have run straight into the hands of the Gestapo.

Why didn't anyone who passed me by before, try to warn me? Very simple. Who was I to them? I could be a collaborator, an informer to the Germans; I could be a German agent. Nothing guaranteed I was a Belgian patriot; how could they take chances?

I changed course, hoping to make enough of a detour to bypass the trap. I succeeded, and made my rendezvous.

I was still working as my father's secretary, and he still had no knowledge of my Resistance activities.

One morning we had unwelcome visitors at the office. My father was dictating to me when one of his employees knocked and opened the door and was immediately pushed aside by a civilian who introduced himself as being from the Gestapo.

I left and walked upstairs to the employees' office. (My father's office was on the mezzanine, the employees' office on the second floor.) A few minutes later, another individual walked into the employees' office and demanded to see my identity card. He scrutinized it thoroughly and returned it without comment, then walked out.

A few seconds later I decided to find out what he was up to, and discovered him searching through a big walk-in closet on the upper mezzanine. I worried for my father then, because in this closet was quite a supply of flour and grain. My father had obtained it on the black market in order to bake some decent bread instead of eating the rationed bread, which, as the months went by, became practically inedible. The black market was, of course, forbidden. But, obviously, and luckily, this was not the reason for the Gestapo's intrusion. The headman stayed with my father for over an hour, then both agents left. We all sighed with relief, but we were apprehensive of what would be the follow-up.

The official reason given for the Gestapo's visit was that they had been notified that my father was sheltering a Jewish girl, and I was the one suspected of hiding there under a false identity. They left satisfied that this report was a mistake.

Harassment grew, however. Organized groups of collaborating hoodlums went on vandalism forays, obviously with specific targets. One Sunday noon it was Father's home that was on their agenda. I wasn't present, but the incident was related to me by my father. The family—my father, his wife (my stepmother), my stepsister and her fiancé (a cousin)—were having dinner when they heard shouting down the street. This was totally unusual in this quiet residential neighborhood. The brouhaha came closer.

Suddenly the group appeared, massing in the middle of the street, calling my father's name followed by invectives and all sorts of insults. The dining room faced the street, and had a big picture window. As is the fashion in Europe, the ground floor windows were protected at night by heavy wooden shutters that rolled down from the inside. The young cousin realized the imminent danger, jumped up from the table, and as quickly as possible rolled down the shutter. The mob surged forward, trying to prevent the operation, but luckily their efforts failed, even when they tried to pry the shutter up with crowbars.

But they had apparently brought along some kind of ram, and started attacking the front door with that weapon. Although not a big one, the door was of solid oak, and heavy. They succeeded in breaking the door open, but as they were about to invade the house there was a sudden halt, then flight. At the entrance to the street had appeared a German uniformed contingent.

It turned out that a neighbor had called the German authorities when he saw what was happening. Although their arrival at the scene certainly saved my father's home from ransacking or worse, there always remained the suspicion that this had all been orchestrated with the knowledge of the German authorities.

This intrusion by the Gestapo had a visible effect on my father. He seemed to become more apprehensive, and understandably so. He recently had had a speaker system installed at the front door, similar to those found at the entrance of apartment houses in the United States. But it was quite rare in Belgium at this time, and practically unheard of in private, single-family residences. My father had ordered the system to connect with his office. A buzzer would ring in the employees' office upstairs and the caller could be identified before entrance was permitted. But the Gestapo did not identify themselves, and used a fictitious name instead. So, the sense of security my father had expected to achieve by his installation was totally shattered by their intrusion.

Nazi arrests and the taking of hostages increased. One of the victims was a man for whom my father had deep respect, admiration, and friendship. The gentleman was a prominent citizen in Antwerp, and resided in a beautiful residential area of town. The news of the horrible deed hit like a bombshell. We were stunned.

The tragedy unfolded as follows. It was evening, around dinner time, seven or eight, I think. The gentleman's butler responded to the doorbell, opened the front door, and was forcefully pushed aside by two SS agents who stormed in the hallway demanding to know where the owner was. At that point the wife appeared at the top of the stairs, inquiring what this was all about. The two agents hurried up the staircase and harshly asked the lady of the house where her husband was. She responded that he was in the bathroom, and would be available in a couple of minutes. They brushed her aside and rushed to the bathroom. A few seconds later there was a shot, followed by the reappearance of the two SS agents who, without a word, rushed down the steps, and out the door. They had shot the husband in cold blood!

The slaughter of this gentleman for no apparent reason affected my father deeply.

Our sabotage group missions continued to increase, and the need for a source of supply close at hand became urgent. Therefore, I was asked to set up a sub-depot at my home.

The closest big depot was in Malines, as mentioned before. There a Belgian patriot who was in the building business had part of one of his warehouses used as a repository for the metal drums which were flown from England and parachute-dropped at night.

One morning Victor, the chief saboteur, was waiting in my apartment for the arrival of a panel truck with twelve of those drums from the depot in Malines. The appointed time arrived, then passed, but nobody showed up. As the minutes, then an hour, went by, anxiety for the fate of this truck and its driver grew. Had he been stopped with his dangerous cargo? In that case he would be interrogated and, without doubt, manhandled to make him talk. Would he be able to feign ignorance, or would he crack under the abuse?

Victor became more and more restless, and finally declared we couldn't wait any longer. Explosives were needed for a mission that evening and another the following day, so Victor decided we would go to Malines ourselves and find out whether the truck had been there or not.

A couple of hours later we arrived at the depot. There had been no sign of the truck and no call from the driver; only silence. We waited anxiously for another hour, then Victor instructed me to go back to Antwerp by train, taking a couple of bags filled with the explosives and accessories. He would wait a little longer, still hoping for the arrival of the truck. He would contact me later at home.

The electric trains from Brussels to Antwerp, which stopped at Malines, ran about every thirty-five minutes, but the station was virtually deserted. I walked onto the platform, clutching my bags, which were quite heavy, but handling them as if they were featherweight, also as if they were non-essential. Two or three other commuters appeared on the platform. Then two Germans in civilian clothes.

How did I know they were Germans?

The Gestapo—to just mention one type of agent who quite often wore civilian clothes—were usually obvious to us. Was it their physical appearance? Their features? Their mannerisms? Or a combination of the three? Whatever it was, we could generally pick them out; and the two individuals who suddenly appeared at the platform door, were, without doubt, two of them!

More than ever I had to play it cool. I remained standing in the same spot for a couple of minutes and glanced at them casually, not showing more interest in them than in the other three commuters standing some thirty feet away. But the two bags really started weighing on me. With apparent nonchalance, I paced up and down along the platform a couple of times, then put the bags down. I opened my handbag and, continuing my casual behavior, proceeded to refresh my makeup, powdering my nose and retouching the lipstick.

The two German agents had left their spot near the entrance and were walking down the platform. Was this the dreaded moment? In the next two or three seconds, would they halt in front of me, and would I hear the words, *"Gestapo. Ihre Papieren!"* commanding me to show my identity papers. Then they would order me to open my bags. But they only strolled by, scrutinizing me as they passed.

Continuing my act of casual behavior, I left my two zippered bags filled with explosives and walked several feet toward the edge of the platform and peered down the railroad tracks, displaying interest in the train's eventual arrival. Then, just as nonchalantly, I came back toward my two deadly bags. I picked them up, and moved toward where the three other commuters were waiting.

It seemed an eternity before the train finally rumbled into the station and came to a stop. It was good to plop down in one of the seats and relax for a few minutes. But it was a shallow relaxation. Even if there were no inspection aboard the train, I certainly faced the danger of a search on disembarking. One never knew where they would hit, of course.

I debated mentally whether to get off at the Central Station in Antwerp and cross a much-traveled part of town back to my apartment, or to disembark at a little station in Vieux-Dieu, a suburb of Antwerp. I hesitated until the last possible moment, when the train halted in Vieve Dieu, then jumped off the train just as it was about to leave. My decision had been a good one! No Gestapo was to be seen; the little station was deserted except for the Belgian official who took my ticket stub.

It was a beautiful sunny day, but I had to get home without delay; Victor would be coming later to pick up some of the explosives for the missions that had to be accomplished. I was several kilometers from my apartment, and although the station was at the terminus of the line which served my area, there was no streetcar in sight. So I set out on foot—a safer way anyhow, in light of the cargo I was carrying; streetcars were not checked as a rule, but one never knew.

I made it back to my apartment without any further alerts, and anxiously awaited either news or a visit from Victor. I was eager to know what had happened to the pickup truck and the driver who was to have delivered the explosives that morning. An hour or so went by, then the doorbell rang. I peeked through the front window and saw the pickup truck below, parked at the curb. I rushed down, and Victor announced they had the load.

A quick unloading plan was established. The driver and Victor would take the metal drums out of the panel truck and bring them through the front garden, then hand them to me to lug them as quickly as possible down the wooden stairs into my private coal cellar—which, of course, contained no coal whatsoever! My muscular strength and speed certainly came in handy in moving this load down the stairs.

Twelve big drums were now stacked in my cellar. I locked the door, and rushed back upstairs, anxious to hear the story about the delay.

As I reached the front door, the panel truck was already driving away. Victor closed the little wrought-iron gate of the garden, and hurried inside.

Back upstairs in my third-floor apartment Victor told me that shortly after I had left the depot the truck had arrived. All our worry had been for naught; mechanical trouble had been the reason he did not make the rendezvous with us that morning. The drive back, luckily for them, had gone unhindered.

Looking back at the unloading we had just completed, we couldn't help finding humor in the situation. As I mentioned before, several apartment buildings and private homes in my neighborhood had been requisitioned by the Germans, and were occupied by Luftwaffe personnel. So, while we were unloading these metal drums which had been parachuted in to occupied Belgium by the Allies and whose contents were all destined to sabotage German installations, the German Luftwaffe airmen were walking by on the sidewalk in front of my home!

We proceeded to assemble all the necessary materials for the different charges needed for the job that night, and Victor went on his way.

The following day I went down into the cellar to reassure myself that the neighbor living on the ground floor could not spot the drums in my cellar. There was a grating covering a window-well which let light into my cellar; but this grating was situated on the back porch of the ground-floor apartment, and I was convinced that the neighbor would snoop around. He had given me proof of that on previous occasions, and super-caution was a must. Several days later, however, I caught him in the act, but I never let on. He didn't realize that I was in the cellar, and I remained perfectly still in a far corner in the dark cellar as I watched him peering from every possible angle above.

7 As the months turned into years, the German war machine continued its relentless path of destruction and its growing demand upon the population of occupied Belgium. Not only food, but all other necessities became scarcer for us.

Coal was practically unavailable. I, for one, had none of the precious commodity in my cellar. I didn't have the financial means at that time to order any, and even if I had, the chance of getting it was very meager.

The winter was bitterly cold, one of the coldest we had had for many years. Entering my apartment was like opening the door of a freezer. The apartment house was equipped with central heating, but the owner, just like the rest of the population, was unable to get coal.

Because of the cold dampness the wallpaper in my bedroom started separating from the wall near the ceiling, and hung pitifully curled downward. The side panel of my beautiful wardrobe, a lovely piece of furniture, was wet to the touch! At night I shivered in this cold, damp environment, despite the multiple layers of blankets.

Mitsy, my faithful black cat, shared this misery with me. She had a daily routine. When I gave the signal to go to bed, I would say: "Mitsy, dodo!" (An affectionate term; "dodo" meaning *dormir,* to sleep.) On cue, Mitsy would trot toward the bedroom, jump up on the window sill there, and would only come down from her perch when I was tucked in and had turned out the light. I would hear the thump of her jumping on the parquet floor, then she would jump up onto the bed, pawing the cover about a foot from my face as if to say, "Lift the comforter," which I did. Then she would curl up between the comforter and the blanket, close to me, and go to sleep.

A friend of mine, who was also a friend of my father's, visited me and was appalled at my living conditions. During the first winter of the German occupation he had brought me an old-fashioned stove, which we installed in my living room. Already central heating was unavailable. With this stove it had been wonderful; it had been warm and cozy. But, of course, the day came when my little reserve of coal was exhausted, and thus the present misery came to be.

Thinking he was doing me a favor, my friend notified my father of my lack of heating, expecting I would get help from him. But the result was a disaster. I was strongly berated, then given an ultimatum: I was to stay overnight at Father's home until coal could be obtained! This, I repeat, was a disaster for me! It hindered my Resistance activities, which were still completely unknown to the family and had to remain that way. In addition, the feeling toward me in the parental home was miserable, to put it mildly.

My father contacted his coal merchant, and after a week of repeated reminders I was promised a delivery and released from confinement in my family's home.

No matter how parsimoniously I used the precious coal, it didn't last forever. Luckily, I was able to acquire some wood, but this turned out to be a non-solution when the wood wouldn't burn! I had been the victim of one of those profiteering merchants who used every possible dishonest means to make money. This entrepreneur was selling wood which he had soaked, so as to augment the weight, for wood was sold by the kilogram.

Another time I was able to buy some tree roots. This was another experience! The pieces were much too big for the stove, so they had to be cut. I tried to hack them, to saw them, but it was like hitting cement. The neighbor from the apartment just below me witnessed my hopeless efforts one day as he came down into the cellar, and insisted on doing it for me, but he was just as unsuccessful. After hours of the most strenuous efforts, I was finally able to reduce these hunks to a usable size!

Ever since I was a child, my hands and feet suffered greatly during the cold winter months. Both would crack and bleed. And now, under the extreme living conditions imposed on the Belgian population by the German occupier, this situation was at its worst. My heels cracked open; wide gashes formed and bled. I tried to dampen the pain I felt at every step by swathing the base of the heel in a layer of cotton wool. But the worst were my hands. Cracks appeared at my finger tips on both sides of the nails. It was excruciatingly painful to pound these fingers on the typewriter. I will never forget how one day I typed my reports with gloved hands! It was the only way to soften the contact with the keys and to be able to endure the pain.

These hardships, shared by all the Belgian people, only increased the hatred for the German occupier, the cause of all these shortages, and fueled the craving to destroy the enemy.

To add to the dismal atmosphere there was the imposition of blackout. Ever since the start of the German occupation, total blackout had been imposed. No light was to show at night.

My big picture window in the living room, which gave out on the front of the house, had voile curtains and heavy drapes. Over these were a contraption I had put together, consisting of two wooden slats with heavy black paper stretched between them. Hooks at each end of both slats fit over nails I had pounded into the wooden valance near the ceiling. I hooked one slat on one nail, unrolled the paper, and hooked the second slat to the second nail on the other side. I rolled this screen up during the day and laid it down on the floor below the window, and put it up again at dusk, and so, "blackout" was assured! Necessity brought out ingenuity in all of us!

Failure to observe the blackout was punished by the occupier with fines or arrest, and sometimes the windows were even shot out by German patrols. I made sure no light was visible outside. Because of my activities, I couldn't afford to be exposed to a visit by the patrols!

The blackout applied also on the streets; street lights stayed off, and cars and bicycles had to have their lights covered, letting only a thin sliver of light shine through. When I was riding my bicycle through the dark streets on my missions, I felt doubly on the alert; the slightest movement springing out of the dark took on such bigger proportions. The feeling of imminent dangers was doubly present!

8 By now I was not working for my father anymore. My stepmother had finally achieved the goal she had worked toward from the start: permanent severance of the bonds between my father and me. If it hadn't been for the war, this rift probably would not have happened. I probably would have been hurt, but I would have taken whatever abuse I had to. But the war had changed things. I was my own woman, not the obedient, subjugated European daughter. I stood up to the unfair onslaught, and the final break occurred.

From the standpoint of my activities in the Resistance, it was, without doubt, a blessing. My time was my own now; I could go when and where I was needed at a moment's notice.

There was one big concern, however. I had no cash reserve. I had been living—barely—from one paycheck to the other, and now found myself cut off. I inquired after typing work at a reproduction business, and was given a small job. From that moment on I had more work than I had time for. In addition, the son of a friend of my father's contacted me and asked if I would type his thesis. I was thrilled; it was a most interesting job, and I was well paid for it. The young man, who was a perfectionist, was very pleased with my work, which was a double satisfaction.

Not having to commute daily to my father's office was also a blessing, for it gave me a respite from the constant repair of bicycle tires. They were a sight, bulging here and there from the vulcanized patches all over their surfaces. The streets of Antwerp were mostly paved with cobblestones, which caused much wear and tear on the tires. Still, my bike was not the worst-looking of those seen daily on the road. One wondered how some of these bicycles kept their tires inflated, for many had their punctures covered with rags bound around the tire and the wheel. They gave a bumpy ride as well! But we all became ingenious in making do with what was available.

Shoes, for instance, often needed resoling, but no leather was available. We had only an ersatz product which didn't last very long and disintegrated twice as rapidly in inclement weather. That winter I had the good fortune of getting hold of a piece of an old car tire, and my dear cobbler very obligingly carved a pair of soles out of it and put them on my boots. This heavy, thick underpinning was far from elegant, but it certainly gave me a warm, solid base, and was very welcome during the rainy, snowy winter.

Food was becoming scarcer by the day. Beans remained the main available staple, although they were rationed like everything else. A monthly ration of beans could be consumed in one normal meal. But we no longer knew what normal meals were; we had to scrounge for everything.

Rutabagas were another staple quite often available, if not popular. These two basic food products had some rather unpleasant consequences. Both cause a well-known digestive reaction, which was very clearly distinguishable if one had to travel on streetcar platforms. The aroma floating around did not exactly tickle one's nostrils!

The acute lack of food had another rather grim side effect: dogs and cats who roamed the streets disappeared at an alarming rate. When one's hunger reaches the point of starvation, one is not choosy!

The rationed bread had become a heavy, dark gray, gooey mass inside a tough, hard crust. It was practically impossible to cut; the mass would stick to the knife, and one had to scrape it off the blade. If one could make a loaf last a week, a green mold would set between the hard crust and the paste inside. But I ate it anyway!

A few days after the drums of explosives were stored in my cellar, the chief of materiel of Group G brought a case of grenades that had originally belonged to the Belgian Army. This was another very useful weapon. The first to need them was the right arm to the chief saboteur and a young man for whom I had—and to this day have—a great admiration. He was calm, modest, and thorough. A serious worker and no braggard, he did his job without fanfare.

Jan's dedication and devotion to the cause of freedom merits a special mention. He was in constant danger of being betrayed; he was in the incredible situation of having a brother-in-law who was a collaborator of the most despicable type: a member of the Belgian SS. Yes, unfortunately, we had traitors in Belgium, too, and these Belgian SS were despised by the people to the highest degree.

Not only did Jan have a traitor as a brother-in-law, but the two lived in the same apartment building. So, Jan's comings and goings could be witnessed and monitored by the relatives. Sabotage missions we had to accomplish often kept the men out after curfew, which in Jan's case increased the danger tremendously. The Belgian SS did not come under the curfew rules, of course, so Jan could easily find himself in the position of having to face inquiries by his infamous in-law.

Early one evening Jan came to my apartment to collect some grenades for an upcoming mission. It was a beautiful, balmy evening, and I decided to take a breather, and walk partway into town with him. Five or six long blocks separated us from the neighborhood church, which formed the boundary of the commercial district of the area in which I lived. We were about one hundred yards from the church when the bells struck eight. Jan suddenly realized he could not possibly get to his destination before curfew. There was no question of him carrying this load we had assembled. He could not risk being stopped. He wanted to turn back with me and return the grenades to my apartment, but this I absolutely refused to let him do. Instead, I insisted he get on his way immediately, and he reluctantly handed the satchel with the grenades to me and we both went our ways. He would get the grenades in the next day or so.

Jan might have been especially worried about my toting this lethal satchel home so close to curfew. A German contingent had occupied the corner building of my street, and in the block preceding my street was another German post. This was where the Russian prisoners I mentioned before had been billeted, and of course it was a German guardhouse.

They didn't stop me as I gingerly walked by. A few minutes later, as I entered my residence and closed the door, I let out a sigh of relief at having been lucky another day.

Our sabotage missions increased steadily, and with noticeable enthusiasm. The men's confidence in the success of their exploits was obvious, and for good reason. This enthusiasm came blurting out one afternoon when Victor came to get more of the supplies he had asked me to prepare.

He looked radiant. He was excited and exuberant as he told me about the German ammunition train that had been blown up by our explosive charges two days before. The charges had been laid on the tracks, and the success of the mission had been enhanced by the fact that a whole contingent of Nazi military personnel had been eliminated in the same blasts. The German command had attached troop-carrying compartments to the ammunition train, and the result of our mission had this awesome added dividend. "Bodies of soldiers were hanging in the trees," said Victor.

The mission had taken place in the Campine, a wide, mostly uninhabited area north of Antwerp, covered with sandy soil and pine woods alternating with big expanses of briar, which in autumn offer lovely, peaceful expanses of bluish-purple ground cover. This bucolic scene was at that moment shattered by the horror of war. This was a price we had to pay in the fight for freedom.

The German command reacted fiercely to our successful mission. Hostages were taken, and the search for the saboteurs was on in full force. The Germans were determined to leave no stone unturned. Victor voiced his apprehension in no uncertain terms. More than ever, the utmost caution had to be exerted. If we were caught and linked to this mission, the horrors of what might happen to us would have no limits.

A few days later there came a very unsettling piece of news, which affected me personally. The Germans were requisitioning additional properties in my neighborhood. This, of course, involved the inspection of potential buildings.

This new situation called for immediate action. All the explosives had to be removed from my cellar immediately.

In the evening, Hubin, the chief of materiel, came up with another agent, an engineer-chemist, and we went down to my coal cellar and worked at defusing the grenades. It was eerie in the dimly lit corner of my coal cellar where we sat amid the metal drums of explosives silently doing the dismantling job in preparation for the move. Silence was the motto. The neighbor right above my cellar had to remain unaware of our presence.

I was told that the next afternoon we would try to transfer all of the explosives to a new location. The life-threatening question for me now was, could I escape the inspection of my residence by the German command for another day? If not, I was doomed.

As the morning hours went by, tension grew. I kept an anxious ear to every boot stomping on the pavement below and to every activity on the street. Fortunately there was only the usual coming and going of the Luftwaffe. No German inspection team came to survey the premises.

Shortly after noon Hubin arrived, followed a few minutes later by the appearance of a farmer with his horse and wagon. We sprang into action. The metal drums in the coal cellar were slipped individually into potato sacks, and hurriedly stacked in the wagon one by one. The crate of grenades was handled similarly. Then we were on our way.

There had been no time to tell me the exact location where the explosives were to be kept. I only knew that we were heading for Elsdonck, a suburb a few miles to the south. The road we had to take passed right in front of an anti-aircraft installation the Germans had dug only yards away from nearby residences, and there were always sentries in front of the batteries. Diversion was called for to distract attention from the farmer's horsecart, so I jumped on my bicycle and raced a hundred yards ahead of the loaded wagon. As I entered the stretch leading to the German installation, I changed my pace abruptly to a leisurely rhythm, zig-zagging, and turning figure-eights across the road. As I came abreast of the sentinel, I said *"Schönes Wetter nicht?"* (Nice weather, isn't it?) The guard took the bait; he approached and showed interest in a chat, and I obliged. The important thing was to keep him from any interest in the horse and wagon, which had by now almost caught up with me. I kept up my verbal exchange with the guard until the lethal transport was out of danger, then, jumping back on my bicycle, I reassumed my leisurely peddling until I was out of sight of the guard. Then I quickened my pace and fell in close behind the farmer and his precious cargo.

We finally arrived at the farm. There was not a second lost. In what I assumed to be his dining room, the table was moved aside, the rug rolled up, and a trap-door opened. Hubin, who had been riding with the farmer, and I followed the farmer down, and found ourselves in a secret underground hideout. It had been beautifully reinforced like a mine. Hubin was very pleasantly impressed, and so was I.

The potato sacks containing the metal drums were swiftly taken off the carriage and lugged into the underground cache. Then the trap door was closed, the rug spread over it, and the table put back on top of it all.

Our supplies were safe for the time being!

9 I had been an avid reader ever since childhood. But a peculiar thing happened to me after the few first months of being involved in the Resistance. One evening, in the winter of 1941–42, I was huddled near the stove reading a novel by one of my favorite French authors. I had been able to get some wood on the black market and it was crackling nicely and putting out some needed warmth. Suddenly I stopped; my eyes had read a whole page, but my mind hadn't retained one thought. I tried to shake off what I thought was sleepiness, and started the page all over, but to no avail. I could not retain a thing of what I was reading. Disgusted, I went to bed.

The following day the same thing happened, and on many subsequent tries at reading as well. Was it because my mind was too preoccupied with my present activities, or too much on the *qui vive*? I don't know what it was, but the joy of reading novels remained an impossibility, and to this day I have not regained my former avidity.

My second joy was music, and I turned more and more to my piano in search of mental satisfaction. Classical music was a big outlet for me. Beethoven, Mozart, Haydn, Mendelssohn, Schubert, Schumann, Chopin . . . sonatas, études, impromptus: they gave such an outlet! And it was not only piano playing, but also singing in which I found such pleasure. There my repertoire consisted mainly of the *lieder* of Schubert and Schumann, as well as a few opera arias. I also enjoyed Negro spirituals tremendously. I was a big admirer of Marian Anderson; I was also a contralto, and could imitate her style to a T. Unfortunately, however, the English language was forbidden in any shape or form by the German authorities. I was asked by the president of the tennis club I belonged to, to sing at a party that was being planned. I agreed, and told him that I would sing Negro spirituals. The answer immediately was: "Oh, no! That is forbidden! They couldn't risk this!" One of the members was a "collaborator," and thus the risk of being denounced was great.

I told him it would be Negro spirituals or nothing, and he had better look for someone else. A few days later, however, I was told that the board of directors had decided to take the risk! I was delighted. This was an opportunity publicly to project defiance of the Nazi occupier, and to create a pro-Ally enthusiasm.

The evening of the performance there was some anxiety on the part of the organizers because, as feared, the collaborator-member was present.

His presence produced the opposite effect in me, however, and I gave it my all. The membership responded with enthusiasm. And at the conclusion of the program, the collaborator came over especially to congratulate me! He obviously did not report us to the German authorities, because no action was forthcoming.

My music did, however, cause some unpleasant—to put it mildly —and dangerous happenings.

In my mail one day I found a letter unmistakably written by a German. The handwriting on the envelope betrayed its origin. What German would know my name?

The letter was magnificently written: the handwriting was beautiful, and the style was outstanding. The writer expressed his admiration for my musical talents, and described with enthusiasm how he listened to my piano playing, to my singing while standing in the street below my window! He even commented on the different compositions I had performed. I was flabbergasted, but even more I was intrigued and concerned how this individual knew my name, and who he could be.

I showed Hubin the missive a couple of days later. He told me not to worry about it, and laughingly complimented me on having such an appreciative audience! However, another letter arrived a few days later, and another, and another . . . all in the same elated style, but with increasing expressions of infatuation for me personally, even describing in flattering terms the clothes I had been wearing!

The mailman happened to make his delivery just as I was leaving the house that day, and handed me an envelope with a special gleam in his eye. He too had recognized the German handwriting. Clearly showing my annoyance at receiving this mail, I asked him, "Whom does this come from?" He smiled in a cunning way and walked away. This, of course, convinced me that *he* had given my name to the writer.

A couple of evenings later, the doorbell rang. I didn't expect anyone and the ring caused the usual apprehension. I opened the door and my heart surged upward when I found myself facing a blue-gray uniform of the Luftwaffe.

No hard command or questions were thrown at me; instead, the man identified himself as the letter writer, and proceeded to reiterate his enjoyment of my music, and expressed his desire to visit with me.

I thanked him for his compliments, but declared in no uncertain terms that I had no intention of starting a relationship, and politely but firmly bid him goodnight, and closed the door.

A few evenings later I was listening, as usual, to the BBC news broadcast—a thing strictly forbidden by the German authorities—when the doorbell rang. I switched the radio to a German-controlled station and hurried down the two flights of stairs. To my dismay I found myself once again facing my Luftwaffe secret admirer.

At first he used the same approach as on his first call. But upon my refusal of his request to visit, he suddenly pushed me aside and went up the two flights to my apartment.

A mixture of feelings welled up in me. I was furious; I was mortified to have an enemy in my home—visiting! I was worried for several reasons. First I feared for the people in the apartment below me. They, too, always listened to the BBC broadcast, and as the gentleman was very hard of hearing he always played it very loudly, and it could be heard in my apartment. Fortunately, on this occasion, the German station I had switched on covered it.

Second, I was not enthralled at the thought of being at the mercy of my neighbors, who, because of this unwanted visitor, might smear my reputation as a Belgian by branding me as a collaborator.

The effrontery of this invasion of my private domain by sheer "right of the oppressor" made me boil. In my delicate position, however, I couldn't afford to cause an upheaval. Still, I was not about to take this intrusion for granted, and expressed myself accordingly.

The man apologized, then proceeded to reiterate his complimentary commentaries. He was obviously very knowledgeable on the subject of music. I don't recall how the conversation shifted to the Russian front and my deliberate but subtle opinion that the Germans faced the risk of defeat. His reaction was explosive, like a Dr. Jekyl–Mr. Hyde transformation, and the Nazi fanaticism and propaganda spurted forth. Fortunately, his unwarranted visit concluded without further incident.

I was imposed upon by this guest two or three times more, the last of them at a totally unexpected hour: pre-dawn! He had to see me again, he said; he had orders to leave town immediately! I tried to get him to tell me what his Luftwaffe contingent's destination was, but he wasn't about to tell.

A couple of weeks later I received a letter, again in the same effusive style, but with increased infatuation. Because it came through the German military postal service, I had no information as to its origin. Hubin instructed me to answer the letter, and to try— indirectly, of course—to find out where the regiment had been transferred.

It was one of the most distasteful tasks I ever performed. I had to deliver the letter at a German military post office. I literally cringed when I set foot in this place, and couldn't get out fast enough. But my discomfort was not for nothing. I did receive a reply, and it contained enough indirect comments for us to pass on the information to the Allies. The area we had pinpointed was confirmed to have had an influx of Luftwaffe, and the Allies bombed it shortly afterwards, with heavy casualties to the enemy.

The Russian front weighed heavily on the Germans, and their morale was sagging. Meanwhile, our activities were redoubled. All power stations, railroad traffic, and nerve centers of all kinds were our targets. Although I didn't have the metal drums filled with explosives in my possession anymore, I would have complete charges brought to me, then I delivered them as in the past. The requisition of my apartment building by the Nazis had not yet come to pass.

I had received a call from Victor requesting materials for a job. I went on foot, and made the delivery without incident. On my return it was seconds before curfew when I hastily rounded the corner of the last block to my apartment. As I have mentioned, the corner apartment building was a German command post, and just as I passed less than ten feet from the entrance, the German patrol walked out to start on their rounds. There were two soldiers accompanied by their two German shepherds. I froze! I had a deadly fear of dogs. My heart was pounding wildly.

The patrol left the sidewalk and started across the square. When they were a few steps away from the curb, one of the dogs faced me and, baring his teeth, growled menacingly. I had often been told that dogs sense fear in humans, and that one should never show fear, so I mustered all my courage and advanced a couple of steps. The dog's menacing attitude increased, and his hackles rose as he advanced toward me.

By now the two soldiers had stopped, and showed real pleasure at my predicament. I wondered when they would sic the dog on me. But suddenly, I heard a barely audible whistle, and the dog relaxed slightly; a second barely audible whistle, and he rejoined his masters. The soldiers made their enjoyment of the episode known with a loud laugh!

If I had had wings I don't think I could have covered the couple of hundred yards to my front door any faster!

Part Three:
Escape Line

1 It was spring of 1944. Three years had gone by since I joined the Resistance. The Germans were now feeling the strength of the Allied bombings over their *Vaterland*. The devastation was tremendous. We loved to hear the heavy bomber squadrons fly over Antwerp on their way to Germany; but how heartbreaking it was to watch the dozens of searchlights sweeping across the black night sky, and suddenly see an Allied plane caught by one of them. Immediately then all the lights converged on the poor lonely flying machine, and it looked like a butterfly trapped in a spiderweb! The tracer bullets converged relentlessly toward him, and the acrobatic maneuvers he performed to try to escape were often in vain. The rat-tat-tat of the German anti-aircraft batteries opened fire from all sides to shoot him down.

This increasing of air-raids by the Allies inevitably brought an increase in Allied casualties. This gave birth to the Escape Line, a network dedicated to sheltering downed Allied airmen and smuggling them back to England.

To my great delight, I was asked to participate in providing shelter for Allied airmen! I had thought my enthusiasm was at its peak after three and a half years in the espionage network, and in our sabotage group. But when this latest request for shelter was made, that enthusiasm shot up a few more notches!

I would like to project the cadre in which this added activity was to take place, and thereby create the ambiance and share the feeling of elation I was experiencing.

My apartment was situated on a wide, tree-lined avenue, and several of the big apartment houses had been taken over by the German military forces. As I have mentioned before, the foot traffic of the Luftwaffe personnel was constant on the sidewalk below. So, the thought of having Allied airmen hidden in my home, peering at the enemy from two floors above, seemed the epitome of wishful thinking. But now, in early May, 1944, it became reality. My excitement in the hours preceding their coming rose and rose.

Three flyers arrived with their escort, who became known to me as Donald. Two were Britishers, of the Royal Air Force (RAF): one was a navigator, John Stanley Woodward; the other, William Lynch, was an engineer aboard a Lancaster, whose targets had been Düsseldorf. The third airman, Leslie Anderson, was a Canadian flying officer of the Royal Canadian Air Force (RCAF). The two RAF men had bailed out over Holland; Leslie Anderson, the Canadian, had bailed out over Belgium.

They were three quite different types. Stanley Woodward, the navigator, was young in spirit and in looks. He was small in stature, thin, with a most pleasant personality. Bill Lynch, the engineer, was very reserved, mature in appearance and spirit, it seemed. Leslie Anderson, the Canadian, was a quite different individual. He was a lanky man of few words, but they were always to the point, quite often with a sharp, wry sense of humor.

The Escape Line extended into Holland. The men were transferred from shelter to shelter, some going by train or trolley car, others by road on bicycles. One of our agents escorted and led them.

The first item of extreme importance was to provide them with false identity papers before they set off on their journey. In Belgium, all citizens over fifteen years of age were obliged by law to carry an identity card with a photograph at all times. Under the German occupation, observance of this rule was of the highest importance. Non-compliance would have been more dangerous, and one could not afford to move about without an identity card.

The airmen were also provided with civilian clothes. These clothes were not exactly the latest fashions, but consisted of whatever could be gathered from people supporting the cause.

The British engineer and the Canadian flying officer looked quite presentable, but the young navigator was wearing a pair of pants that looked about four sizes too big in the seat! After a couple of days, I decided that it would be good for his morale to get him into some better-fitting trousers, ones in which he didn't need to make double folds in the waist.

In the closet I had a dark blue suit that belonged to my husband, who was now in America. He, too, was of a very slim build. This nicely tailored suit made our young man look like a different person, and his morale rose.

I had one bedroom in this small apartment, with a big king-size bed. It was an unusually large bed for that time, but it certainly came in handy in my Escape Line activity. Three men could sleep there, or one, if he preferred, could stretch out on the big sofa in the living room. In that case, I slept out on the floor in my den. So the available lodging, although not providing facilities equal to those at the Ritz, was adequate.

Food was a different story! We were rationed to the point of bare existence; there were monthly ration coupons, but no merchandise for most of them. The black market was our source of nourishment, and a welcome institution in our daily lives. This may sound criminal, but one must consider what the black market represented

Leslie Anderson and William Lynch (behind)

at that time. It was not an exploitation of the masses; it was a risk the farmers took of hiding part of their crops or livestock from the Germans (who collected them for their own use), and then clandestinely sold—at a great risk—to the Belgian population.

We did pay high prices for whatever products we could get from such sources, and they were rather sparse. One could not go in to any shop and get something from under the counter; one had to know someone through a friend, and the exchange was made in private.

So, in the weeks that followed, and for every airman entrusted to my care, my biggest concern was to provide the necessary food.

The presence of these three Allied airmen in my home brought me great joy. By now, we in Belgium had been under the heel of the

Leslie Anderson, William Lynch, and John S. Woodward

Nazi occupation for four years, and I had been active in the Resistance for a little over three and a half years.

The constant fear of being arrested was now pushed to the back burner; my little apartment seemed to be a haven. But this didn't mean we could lower our guard. If we Belgian shelter providers were caught, the death penalty would be our fate. For me this was nothing new! My work as an intelligence agent and my activities in the Group G also carried the death penalty.

However, with these three Allied airmen in my care, there were delightful hours of talk. The airmen were not allowed to give me any military detail, and I was not allowed to ask them any such questions in that field, nor where they had been since bailing out of their disabled planes. But they told some stories about their frightening experiences abandoning disabled, flaming, or powerless aircraft. I marveled at the courage it must have taken to make that jump knowing that they would land in enemy territory if they were lucky enough not to be mowed down by the Nazi troops during their descent. If they did touch down safely without landing in the midst of a Nazi deployment, they had then to face the big unknown: would they be lucky enough to meet helpful natives who would hide them from the enemy?

My first three men had obviously overcome these hurdles, and were now on their way to a base in England. It would be a slow and risky journey, but hopefully a successful one.

These were the things we talked about. I drank up every word, and lived with them the fear, panic, and hope they had experienced.

But here, in my apartment, they seemed to find some rest from those anxieties. Maybe it was the bright home with its whole wall of glass looking out onto the tree-lined avenue below. I treasure a picture of them standing behind the voile curtains, watching the coming and going of the Luftwaffe personnel on the sidewalk below.

One of our top men, active both in the espionage network and in Group G, was Father René Leclef, a Catholic priest, administrator, and professor at St. Stanislas College in Berchem (the suburb of Antwerp where I lived). From now on he became a regular visitor to my home whenever I had Allied airmen in my care, for he spoke English fluently. I would tell him on the phone that I had "a couple of rations" for him. Double talk was always necessary, for there was a constant risk of having the telephone line tapped.

Father Leclef was a marvelous person of incredible stamina, both physical and mental. He had a marvelous sense of humor, and he brought great mental uplift to my airmen. Only after the end of the war did I learn that he, too, had sheltered airmen, and had escorted them from the Dutch border to Antwerp—a very risky assignment. His Resistance work also included distribution of clandestine publications, acting as an intelligence agent, maintain-

Max MacGregor and Louis Rabinowitz

ing contact with the British air-drop units supplying material to the Resistance, surveying potential drop sites, meeting with our chief saboteur to study and plan sabotage missions, and meeting with parachuted British agents.

My three airmen stayed with me for four or five days, until their escort came and fetched them to take them on the next leg of their journey and their next hideout. How I hated to see them go!

But I had no time to feel the loss, for the activities of Group G had not let up, and I still had rent to pay, plus the telephone, and other household expenses, including food! My typing jobs were still fundamental to my survival; I had to hold on to my living quarters in order to maintain my Resistance activities.

A few days went by, then Donald called me, telling me he had two other little "packages" for me. They arrived a couple of hours later. One, Max MacGregor, was a slim, reserved, very gentleman-like young fighter pilot from New Zealand. The second, Louis Rabinowitz, a native of New York, was more ruggedly built, jovial, and extroverted. He was a flight engineer aboard a United States Air Force bomber. In the four years since the war began, I don't think I had laughed as much as during the few days these two men were with me, all due to the witty repartee and crazy doings of my New Yorker! They were both lovely individuals, but utterly different in appearance, mannerism, and background. Their contrast made a good study in human behavior. Once again, they were with me for about five days before Donald took them away.

2   Group G's activity was on the increase again. Although I no longer had the big cache of explosives in my cellar, I still had smaller quantities of munitions hidden in paper bags behind a sofa in my study, and in my kitchen broom closet, behind the pails and cleaning supplies. They were always ready for immediate delivery, and they were in great demand.

There was something in the air, a feeling of something about to happen. There was a tension, not exactly visible, but manifested in various ways more felt than seen.

The German military did not give the appearance of victorious masters anymore. Now the air of the victor was replaced by a subdued, even downtrodden composure. Their physical appearance, too, had taken a complete turn. Their uniforms looked tired; their walk, once proud and determined, was now forlorn; the songs they sung while marching didn't have the rhythmic, forceful cadence of the early occupation days, but was now forlorn and weak.

The other occupation forces—the infamous SS, the Gestapo, etc.—didn't project any such signs, however. To the contrary, their forays increased. They invaded private homes, and arrested Belgian citizens at all times of the day and night. Their brutality and sadism as they interrogated the poor souls who were their victims seemed to have no limit. Reports of electric torture devices made chills run up and down one's spine.

On June 6, 1944, I had a surprise visit from Victor, the chief saboteur. He hadn't phoned in any request for explosive charges, but he seemed very excited. As soon as he set foot in my apartment, he blurted out, "They have landed! The Allies have landed! The invasion has started!"

What fantastic news! And what a fantastic feat for the Allied high command to keep this fantastically large operation so completely secret and take the Germans by surprise!

We felt like shouting this news to the winds!

Victor made his visit a very short one, and took some of the sabotage materiel with him. More than ever, there would be work to be done. More than ever was it important to disable the German lines of communication—power stations, railroads, facilities, etc.

After his departure I, too, left the house, and followed my regular route down the long block, then left on Avenue Elizabeth, right past the German command post. I practically danced as I passed in front of them, unable—in fact not wanting—to hide my elation! I felt like thumbing my nose at them!

That evening I was glued to the radio, listening to the forbidden BBC, as the invasion was announced. What emotional moments those were!

Liberation was coming!

Hubin dropped by late one afternoon to tell me someone would come the next day and drop off a radio transmitter which I was to keep for a few days until it was picked up by another agent. The following day a big square package, about two feet by two feet wrapped in brown paper, was delivered, and I placed it in my den.

Hubin had also asked me if I would accept some airmen from a second source. Needless to say, my answer was an enthusiastic affirmative! To give as much help as I could possibly muster to these brave young Allied airmen was my goal!

Gurth Webster (left) and Len Collins, RAF wireless operators

A few days later I received the eagerly expected phone call, and I was offered "two little rations." They arrived in late afternoon or early evening. They were Len Collins of London, and Gurth Webster of Wales. Like their comrades who had stayed with me earlier, they were both charming, but in quite different ways. This evening, however, they were both quite shaken, and for a good reason. For five days they had been holed up in a single room somewhere in Brussels, not allowed to move around and forbidden to speak above a whisper. This alone was reason enough to have one's nerves raw; being constantly on the qui vive can bring one's nerves to the brink of snapping.

There must certainly have been very solid reason for such discipline. The Belgian citizen in whose home they had been hidden might, for instance, have been obliged by the Germans to turn over part of his home to them, in which case the constant presence of the enemy on the premises would have required those rules. Another reason could simply have been that the owner of the house had, among his visiting friends or relatives, some who were sympathizers to the German regime. In any case, the presence of the Allies had, at all cost, to remain a secret in every sense of the word.

After five days hiding in Brussels, the airmen made the fifty-five-kilometer trip to Antwerp by car. Just as they were about to turn off the Brussels-Antwerp highway onto my avenue, they were stopped by the Gestapo, and asked for their papers. With horror they realized that one basic task had been overlooked: to provide the men with false identity papers before leaving Brussels.

Luckily their escort, in keeping with his solid character and training, rallied to the emergency. He was seated in front, next to the driver; the two escapees were in the back seat. Pretending to accept their identity cards as he turned toward them, the escort instead slipped two false cards out of a packet he was carrying and, adding his own genuine one, handed them over to the Gestapo.

Luckily for them, the German was more interested in the official stamps applied than in the photographs; returning the cards, he let them pass.

This was a close call! When they arrived at my apartment, five minutes later, the airmen were still quite shaken, especially the one who was Jewish, who said, "If they catch me, they won't arrest me as a prisoner of war; they will arrest me as a spy!" Depending into whose hands he fell, this might very well have been the case; if so, he would have been executed.

Once again, my joy at having some Allied airmen in my home was immense. I broke a rule that evening. We were supposed to keep the men entrusted to us nicely tucked away, and we were not supposed to take them out of their hiding places. However, that evening I took it upon myself to break that rule. I felt it was necessary to create a calmer atmosphere around them, and so I suggested we go out for a walk. They couldn't believe I was in earnest, but when I convinced them I was, they agreed enthusiastically.

We walked down the two flights of stairs and crossed the hallway without encountering any neighbor. Now, all that separated us from the danger zone was a small front garden and its little iron gate.

We set forth on the sidewalk, arm in arm, in the direction of the beautiful big park just a short block away.

As mentioned before, my whole neighborhood was saturated with German military personnel. I could sense the apprehension in my two companions when they spotted the green or gray-blue uniforms of the Wehrmacht and Luftwaffe.

Avenue Royale, where I resided, was a lovely double-double avenue. A sidewalk lined the front gardens; next to it was a cobblestone traffic lane; alongside this was a double tree-lined walkway before the wide macadam roadway, then the reverse to reach the opposite side of the avenue. If some German military personnel were about, they were not always at arm's length.

However, as soon as we reached the park, the situation changed. Now we were to walk on a narrow two-way path.

As the first German came toward us we tensed, but kept a detached appearance; when he greeted us in passing with *Guten Abend* (good evening), the tension relaxed. As we passed other Germans this sequence was repeated with all three of us returning the greetings with our own *Guten Abend,* and the situation took on a humorous slant and clearly relaxed my two young men. It bordered on the incredible: these men who had so lately been shot down by the Germans, were now in occupied Belgium in civilian clothes, rubbing elbows with Luftwaffe personnel who might have been part of the same crew that shot down their plane! But despite our calmed nerves, none of us forgot for one moment that if we were stopped and found out, it would be prison camp for them and the death penalty for me. We headed back home, and reached my apartment once again without bumping into either of my two neighbors.

After a good night's sleep, the airmen faced the new day in a calmer state of mind. Like the previous young airmen, they enjoyed watching the coming and going of the uniformed enemy on the sidewalk below. Then about midday, the doorbell rang. Who could it be? I didn't expect anyone, and the tension was on again. But when I opened the door, there stood Donald with three tall young men. Donald, the usual escort, was bringing three more unexpected airmen. How was I going to lodge them all?

We hurried upstairs. As Donald entered my apartment, he was startled by the presence of my two other charges. "Who are they?" he asked. When I told him they were two other airmen, he asked me in a tone that left no doubt he was upset: "Where do they come from?"

It was my turn to be annoyed and quite astonished, and I replied: "You know the rules: No questions asked!"

Donald left abruptly, announcing he would be back to fetch "his boys" in a few days.

That evening, with five airmen in my small apartment, and only one bedroom, I had a problem. I could accommodate three in my king-size bed, and a fourth on the couch in the living room; I could curl up on the floor in the den. But that left one. I really couldn't expect them to crowd a fourth body in my bed, big though it was!

I pondered, and decided to take a bold move. The neighbors on the floor below me were a nice, quiet family, and without doubt patriotic Belgians and strongly anti-German. I decided to approach them, confide to them who my guests were, and ask if they were willing to provide a sleeping facility in their apartment for the night—maybe for a few nights.

They were overjoyed at the prospect. I told them that I expected the young man to rush back upstairs to my apartment in the morning. I was, of course, very grateful for their help, and was confident they would keep this a secret.

I notified Father Leclef, the wonderful Catholic priest, of the presence of my five guests, and that evening he came on his bicycle and spent an hour or so with us, delighting the young airmen with his warmth and his wonderful sense of humor. Around the table now were Len Collins from London and Gurth Webster from Wales, both RAF pilots who had arrived the day before, and the newcomers brought by Donald, Charles Shierlaw and Lorne Shetler, both Royal Canadian Air Force flyers, and Walter Bush, with the RAF. During the conversation, Charles expressed his great concern

Charles Shierlaw (RCAF) and his wife,
Walter Bush (RAF), and Lorne Shetler (RCAF)

that word of his having been shot down would be reported at home, that he would be declared missing in action. Father Leclef took down some information, and told him he would do his best to have a message reach his family. (After the war Charles reported that the message had, in fact, been received, bringing quite a relief, as one can imagine.)

During the evening, when it came out that two of my Royal Air Force men were wireless operators, I mentioned I had a radio transmitter that was going to be picked up in the next day or so, and they wanted to see if it was in good working order. I fetched it and Gurth and Len spent some time handling it. I felt it was safer not to prolong the experiment, however, and put it away.

Bedtime was upon us, so Walter Bush and I tiptoed silently down the flight of stairs to the first-floor and knocked quietly; the door opened, I whispered again my thanks for the help, and the door closed behind him. We had escaped arousing the curiosity of the ground-floor neighbor. The following morning, as scheduled, I went to get the young man to come back to my quarters.

After breakfast I had to go in search of provisions. As said before, this was not an easy task! How I managed it is hard for even me to conceive after all these years!

Before leaving I had told the men to be careful, not to show themselves at the windows, not to respond to the doorbell or a knock on the door, and to be quiet.

That afternoon, the radio transmitter was picked up.

For me, the presence of these Allied airmen was the most heart-warming experience. My whole self went out to them. For four years we had been under the yoke of the Nazis, and these young men were part of the liberation forces we were so looking up to! In my small apartment, all I could offer them was food and shelter, and the warmth from the depth of my heart. I gave them my gratitude for their help, and for that of their more fortunate companions who could continue their missions of trying to annihilate our common enemy.

I had a piano, and told the men they were welcome to use it, counting on them, of course, not to get carried away in their choice of scores! One could hear the playing very clearly on the street below!

3 A couple of days had gone by when one midmorning the doorbell rang. There stood a young Resistance fighter I knew. He seemed panicky, and breathlessly told me: "You have been betrayed. Get out, they'll be here in an hour!" And off he went, as fast as he could go.

This was the thing I had expected might happen any day ever since I had joined the Resistance. As a matter of fact, more than once I had stated to those who worked with me that if we were arrested, it would mean the end. Our activities drew the death penalty. There was no way to escape it, so, my motto was: if you can't face it, don't start it!

I rushed back upstairs. My only concern was for my five poor airmen. How could I possibly get them out? There was no way. I had no safe place to move them.

My first act was to burn some important papers, first among them a new code I had been entrusted with a day or so before and hadn't yet had the opportunity to pass on. But as I diligently took care of these papers, my mind was still obsessed with the fate of my airmen. They wouldn't be harmed or physically abused, but nevertheless they could not escape to be incarcerated in a prison camp.

I had tears welling up in my eyes, and I tried my best to hide them. But the unusual and obviously frantic activity in which I was engaged, putting the match to papers, didn't escape Charles, the Canadian, who asked me if there were something wrong. I told him there wasn't, and it certainly had nothing to do with them. I obviously didn't convince him, however, and as the minutes ticked by I came to the conclusion that it was better to tell them the truth, and thus prepare them.

Their morale just sank, as expected!

The minutes rolled by; there was practically dead silence in the apartment now. We kept a vigil at the window, where, from behind the curtains, one had a good view of the avenue, and of the sidewalk below.

After about an hour a strange activity started. People were walking two by two nonchalantly back and forth. Some were on the sidewalk adjacent to our front garden, some all the way across the wide avenue on the opposite sidewalk. Some were even in the center strip, sitting on one of the benches under the trees. Never did anyone sit on these benches before!

We checked the back. There was a vacant lot next door which afforded a view of the side and corner of the back street. The same thing was happening there, too! There was no doubt: surveillance was in progress!

A heavy silence seemed to hang over us. I kept busy with my household chores, but our nerves were stretched to the utmost. We watched the minutes, then hours tick by; we continued to watch the guards' actions on the street below. With darkness, our nerves relaxed a bit, and finally we retired for the night.

The following morning we took up our watch from behind the curtains. The same routine was in progress, in front, on the side street, and on the back street.

At mid-morning I had to run the gauntlet to go in search of food for my boys. What was going to happen? Was I going to be apprehended the moment I set foot on the sidewalk? Would they rush forward the moment I opened the front door?

I picked up my bicycle in the entrance hall, opened the front door, and pushed my bicycle to the garden gate. I opened the gate, then, after closing it behind me, I crouched down and pretended to check my pedals and chain, displaying a totally carefree attitude of total unawareness of any crisis or danger. At all cost I had to give that impression, and I obviously succeeded.

I took off, and, as I expected, was followed. But I made my rounds, feigning total ignorance of my shadow as I went from shop to shop in search of food.

Belgium, like most European countries, did not have super-markets of the kind I found in the United States. Food shopping was done daily, with stops at the butcher shop for meat, at the dairy for butter and cheese, and the vegetable shop for all the greens, potatoes, fruit, etc. These shops were not adjacent to each other; far from it. Rather, they were usually several blocks apart. Now, in wartime, one still had to make the rounds in hopes of finding some meager pittance.

I pedaled back home unhindered, and reported to my young men what I had been able to observe, which was, really, not different from what we could see from behind the curtains.

What were they up to? There were at least a dozen agents assigned to our surveillance, leaving little doubt as to their current aim. The Germans had no way of knowing that I had been alerted about the planned arrest. The reason for their delay in executing the order was obvious: they hoped some of my co-workers in the Resistance might come to my home, giving them a chance for a multiple arrest.

We were in our second day of what one could call siege, and our predominant emotion was not fear, nor had it yet reached despair. It was, rather, apprehension, an acute form of it. We took turns watching from behind the curtains, looking for any movement or change in the attitude of our surveillance team, alert to signs of an imminent assault. But everything seemed quiet.

About mid-afternoon, the doorbell rang. We froze; a dead silence enveloped us. Was this the dreaded moment?

I went down the two flights of stairs in no hurry, although my heart was beating at full speed.

I opened the front door and gasped in horror to find Donald standing there. I had only one thought: the danger he was in now!

I urged him in, and whispered emotionally to him—always careful of the occupant of the ground-floor apartment—"We are under surveillance, and have been for two days now!"

Donald showed deep concern, and hurried upstairs. Once in my apartment, he handed me a beautiful bouquet of long-stem roses he was carrying. The gift was most unusual, and quite unexpected. Then, turning to the three airmen he had brought to me a few days earlier, he told them in a tone that did not call for any discussion that he was taking them out, *now!*

Donald proceeded to lay out his plan in a hurried and authoritative manner. In view of our siege condition, we did not expect him to follow his routine procedure, which was to walk out with the men.

The plan was as follows. Two of the men would walk to the side street, just to the right of our building, then turn right onto that street. If they were not followed, they were to light cigarettes after turning the corner onto the back street, then proceed along that street to the Grande Chaussée, the highway to Brussels, where Donald would be waiting.

Once the "all clear" signal was given by these two, the third was to leave, this time turning left into my avenue as he went out the front garden, and thus straight through the assembled German plain-clothes agents, to rejoin the others at the same gathering point.

After making sure the men had understood his instructions, Donald left abruptly. Lorne Shetler and Walter Bush chose the first route. Our hearts were pounding. We watched them walking unhindered toward the side street; the time lapse before they reappeared on the side street had seemed long. They kept up their long, steady stride at a normal pace, not hurried. After turning the corner onto the backstreet, they stopped and gave the all-clear signal by lighting cigarettes, then resumed their walk.

It was Charles Shierlaw's turn now. We were doubly worried for him, for he had to walk right through the pack of agents sprinkled all along my avenue. We watched his tall frame bend over to unlatch the low wrought-iron gate. At this precise moment a young girl-friend of mine, who hadn't visited me at home in months, practically collided with him as she directed her steps to enter the front garden. We saw her address him as he attempted to close the gate behind him. She was evidently telling him to leave it open, because she wanted to come in! He smiled, and closed the gate! She looked a little perplexed, and understandably so.

I had one last glimpse of Charles, tall and straight, walking at a steady pace in the direction of the Grande Chaussée.

My girlfriend, Suzy, rang the bell. I was already halfway down the stairs. I greeted her on the doorstep, trying as much as possible to stay inside the doorway, so as to avoid letting outsiders see whom she was visiting. I told her I could not ask her to come up; instead I urged her to leave immediately.

All this was, of course, totally abnormal behavior on my part. But, as mentioned before, no one, not even my father nor my closest friends, knew of my activity in the Resistance. One could not risk exposure by telling friends or relatives of one's activities. If they knew and didn't report it, they would be considered accomplices, and there was always the danger that they would be arrested if a connection were discovered. Even if they were deeply patriotic, they certainly might break under interrogation, and thus betray the resistant. For those reasons I kept my activities completely secret. In the case of Suzy's unexpected visit, I couldn't have let her in, even if we weren't under surveillance, for I still had two Allied airmen hiding in my apartment. But as it was, if she had been seen in contact with me she might have been jeopardized as well.

So, when I asked Suzy to leave immediately, she looked at me, smiled cryptically, and said: "I thought so!" and left.

There was no doubt she had drawn a conclusion from her rather unusual encounter with Charles a few minutes before. As a matter of fact, after the war she told me what had happened. As suspected, she had said to Charles in French, "Don't close the gate, I have to come in here." To her amazement, he flashed his very warm smile, and, nodding to her, closed the gate! Of course, Charles didn't speak French, and hadn't understood one word of her remark!

The atmosphere in the apartment was gloomy. I tried to cheer up my two remaining airmen, but their hearts were heavy, as was mine. Later that evening, I guess my inner strength gave way somewhat, but the warmth shown by my two young men gave me renewed energy.

Ever since the announcement of the imminent arrest, the messages ordering me to leave had reached me several times, by telephone—of course in double-talk—or by courier. I steadfastly refused to obey the order.

The courier was a young woman. She and her sister operated a little family store selling food products, vegetables, fruit, dry goods, etc., and under the pretext of delivering me some of these products, she delivered the orders in person.

She and her sister operated a letter-drop for the Resistance out of their shop. They received messages and passed them on to those concerned. They were, as we all were, risking their lives every second of the day or night.

That early afternoon she came again, ostensibly to deliver a basket of food. As I grabbed the basket, she slipped me a little piece of paper telling me of a place for me to go *with* the two remaining airmen.

That was wonderful news! All we had to do now was get out before the Gestapo came in!

This is a good time to insert a disclosure which came much later, but which will shed light on the events I have just described.

Donald, the airmen's escort, turned out to be a double agent. Eight months after the Liberation of Antwerp, he was arrested in Paris, where he was spotted by one of our men. Donald had been working at the American Red Cross! Our man notified the authorities, and Donald was arrested and brought back to Belgium. He was executed two years later.

He was never repentant. During the first days of his interrogation, he defiantly declared, "You worked for your ideal, I worked for mine: money!" He had turned in to the Germans over seventy Allied airmen and over fifty Belgian patriots, for one thousand francs each!

In retrospect, the beautiful bouquet of flowers he brought me that day was no doubt a signal from him to the German agents stationed in the street! This explains why my three airmen's departure was unhindered.

The hours ticked by with no change in sight. Another day was rapidly coming to an end, but no arrest!

As usual, dusk brought with it the reduction in number of our guards. But we were jerked out of what had become a sort of fatalistic acceptance when the doorbell rang. Had the Gestapo decided to take us away?

I went down the two flights, once again at a slow pace. Opening the door, both relief and apprehension gripped me. Relief, because here stood not the Gestapo, but one of our saboteurs from Group G, Eugène. He was a middle-aged man who ran a little hardware shop. He was a nice family man who worked in the Resistance with his teenage son. But I also felt apprehension of the danger he was facing if he were found with me.

Eugene rushed upstairs and told us he was determined to get us out tonight! We told him we didn't see much hope of success. As he could see, two guards were at their posts on the bench slightly to the left of us, in the tree-lined center lane. We continued to keep a constant vigil from the window.

Action! The couple on the bench, a male and female, were leaving their bench. By stretching our necks as far as possible, we saw them cross the cobblestone way and stand leaning against the wrought-iron fence of the garden next door.

We continued our vigil, but their new location was not easy to keep in sight. Finally we couldn't detect their presence at all anymore, so Eugène rushed downstairs to check firsthand. We were full of hope. Had they gone? Could we slip out?

A couple of minutes went by, then Eugène reappeared, frustrated. The guards were just two or three houses further down the avenue, leaning against the fence there. It was obvious to us that they were waiting for a relief team for the night.

Another few minutes went by, and Eugène rushed back down. We were not manning the observation spot at my window anymore, it was too dark now to be able to distinguish anything on the street below, and certainly not several buildings away. We left the door to my apartment open so as to be able to hear any call from Eugène below.

Suddenly his muffled call came: "Hurry!" I grabbed my handbag and Donald's roses out of the vase. Eugène urged us out. He had just seen the two German guards turn the corner at the far end of the block. We assumed that their relief team was late, and that they had gone forward to meet them.

We rushed down, out the front garden, and turned the corner one hundred feet to our right. I walked arm in arm with Gurth Webster, carrying those long-stemmed roses as if we were going to a party. Eugène walked with Len Collins.

We had no time to lose. We had a good distance to cover, and curfew was not far off. We could not afford to be stopped by a German patrol and asked for our papers!

We went at a steady pace. At the end of the long block, at the back of my apartment building, we turned left on Avenue Elizabeth, which terminated at the big open space leading to the moat (a remnant of World War I days). The road to Brussels, the Grande Chaussée, was on our right. After crossing the wide open space, we came to the Berchem church, which marked the edge of the older part of town.

Across the road was a barracks occupied by German troops. We set forth through the commercial sector, and onward to our destination, still about three miles away. We had to get there before the 9 P.M. curfew.

About twenty minutes later we reached the quiet residential area, a short block, then we took a sharp turn, and about one hundred yards from the corner we reached our goal, thanks to Eugène's help! As soon as we were inside, Eugène left us, anxious to get back to his own home, which was close by.

4   The woman who had opened the door was middle-aged, and rather plain. She lived alone in this three-story house, of which we never saw any other part than the ground floor. The veranda, as we call it in Belgium, which we would call "family room" or "den" in America, is where we spent all our time. This is where we talked, where we cleaned vegetables or peeled potatoes (if there were any to be had), and where we joked and laughed in the lighter moments.

Mrs. V., the owner, did the shopping; I was not to set foot outside. A makeshift bedroom was set up next to the veranda for me and my two flyers. The real bedrooms were upstairs, where Mrs. V. slept.

The next day I had a visit from a couple of my Resistance colleagues; one to find out if everything was all right, the other announcing they would bring me other downed Allied airmen. These flyers were coming through my second source, and had no connection with Donald.

The following day, two Resistance fighters arrived with another flyer, an American pilot named Joseph K. His escorts took me aside and told me they had serious doubts about his identity. His whole behavior had made their suspicions grow. He was very uncooperative, to the point of being antagonistic. He had been questioned, as were all downed flyers. The Escape Line had to be very careful and on the alert for possible infiltrating Germans posing as Allied airmen.

The two agents burdened me with a heavy responsibility: I was to test him, question him without letting him feel I was checking him out, and watch his reactions, and decide if he was genuine. "Your decision will be the final one. If the report is negative, and he is a German plant, he'll be disposed of!" This was an assignment I didn't cherish!

Joseph K. didn't make the assignment easier. He was completely different from any of the airmen I had had in my care before. He was unpleasant, abrupt, and uncommunicative. He didn't speak a word, and answered only in monosyllables. At times he was outright rude. Furthermore, unlike the other airmen, he wouldn't lift a finger to help in any way. All he did at day's length, regularly, was to stretch out and read. When asked to lend a hand, he barked or mumbled that he had a back pain from his crash landing, then would continue to read. This caused a well-deserved outburst from Len Collins, who told him off in no uncertain terms.

My attempts to initiate any conversation with Joseph K. met with silence or antagonistic reaction. I wasn't getting anywhere. As a matter of fact, I started having my fill of him as well. After all, we were risking our lives to try to help him, and he treated me as if I were dirt!

I had to give my report on Joseph K. in a day or two. I decided to take Gurth Webster into my confidence, and asked him to do his best to question the suspected pilot on technical matters, and to find out, if possible, whether Joseph was genuine.

During mealtime, Gurth forced such a discussion, but it wasn't fast-flowing conversation. Joe's reluctance persisted. However,

Gurth handled it very well, and obtained then and in subsequent exchanges a rather positive assurance that Joe was not an impostor.

The agents arrived that evening, and I gave them our evaluation. The pilot was spared, and remained under my care, but the circumstances under which he had come into the Escape Line continued to be studied. I must say with regret that Joe's uncooperative and outright rude and antagonistic attitude toward me continued all through his stay. He was one sour apple in a bushel of sweet ones!

That evening I was in for a surprise as well. The agents asked me not to forget to keep a record of the expenses I incurred in feeding the airmen. I answered that Mrs. V. was doing the shopping and she could provide receipts. But I was astonished, and asked if this was something new. "What is new?" they asked me. I said, "To be reimbursed." No, was their response. "Haven't you been reimbursed before?" I told them that Donald had never mentioned it, nor asked for accounts, nor offered to help me out financially. I had taken for granted that I was to pay expenses out of pocket, and had even sold some jewelry to be able to do so.

At our hideout there was a little garden surrounded by whitewashed brick walls, typical for this type of residence. We could venture outside there, for the neighbors could not see into it. The weather was very nice, mostly sunny and pleasantly warm. Some of the men took advantage of it, and sat outside. But mostly it was really a dull life for these poor souls whose freedom, and in fact existence, hung on a thread of hope.

There was something about our hostess, the owner of the house, that was worrisome. From her own remarks and from her reports of her conversations when she returned from her shopping expeditions, it seemed she had a need to talk to others with an air of mystery. We suspected she could not keep a secret.

To my amazement, one of the airmen approached me on the subject, and expressed his concern about her apparent lack of discretion. He was quite upset. I tried to assuage his worry. All I could do, and did, was to instill in her the absolute need for total secrecy. I also related our concern to Hubin, who was a regular visitor.

Another visitor one afternoon was François Smout, a fellow agent from the intelligence network. He reported that the news of the Escape Line was not good. The line seemed completely blocked at the moment due to battles on French soil and the increased attention of German intelligence to our operations. Numerous shelter providers and helpers were being arrested. There was obviously an informant in our midst somewhere along the lines.

François promised he would come back shortly, hopefully with better news.

A few days later, on my birthday, June 24, I received a lovely present: another escapee was brought to me. Dennis Belshaw was a young, smiling, good-natured Englishman, an engineer aboard a Lancaster. His squadron's target had been the Ruhr. Dennis had been hit by German anti-aircraft fire over the target area, and had bailed out over Belgium on his return flight.

Dennis Belshaw at the hideout, June 1944 (left), and after the war.

We had an unexpected visitor, who came with two of the regular agents the next evening. He was a monk, and a devoted, diligent worker in the Escape Line. His main activity was along the Holland–Belgium border, where he picked up escaped flyers and escorted them down the network. He would pedal with them on bicycles along the rural roads from the border to some village hideout inside Belgium, or escort them by train or streetcar to a pre-arranged shelter. Some of my charges had been in his care, and they were quite pleased to see him again.

He was quite a figure in his hooded vestment with the rope around his waist and the sandals on his feet, and he threw an aura of mystery over the scene as he sat on the dimly lit veranda, like part of a *mise-en-scène* for a stage play!

I was glad to have François visit me again a couple of days later. Unfortunately, the news he brought was still bad; everything was at a standstill now, the Escape Line more than ever blocked. However, he gave me a contact in Brussels, where there might be a slim chance of getting through.

I decided to risk leaving the hideout. The boys were getting restless, and I felt I had to try this possible lead.

I dressed like a charwoman in an old coat provided by our hostess, which hung on me like an old rag. I wound a scarf around my head like a turban, completely hiding my hair, and off I went. I went straight to the central station in the center of town, bought my ticket, and marched through the huge hall, then up the wide stone steps to the train platforms.

The German military were quite prominent as they moved about the station. I located my train, and hurried aboard. The half-hour journey to Brussels went without incident. No searches, no identity checks.

In Brussels I had quite some ground to cover to get to the location of my contact, but it turned out to be for naught. The escape route there was also blocked. What were the prospects? No one, of course, could predict. So many things were involved. Many arrests had been made, couriers had been ambushed, and hiding places had been raided. There was a leak somewhere.

Disappointed by the failure of my mission, I headed back to the station, but suddenly decided to stop first at one of the big department stores to get a few personal items for each of the men.

I had already purchased a couple of small items when my sixth sense signaled a warning. I casually looked toward adjacent counters, scanning the area, and there to my right was the cause.

A typical German agent—in civilian clothes of course—stood about fifty feet away, staring at me.

I pretended not to have noticed him, and nonchalantly moved to another counter, faking interest in a couple of articles there. The agent followed me, standing again a short distance away, and from the corner of my eye I noticed a second agent fifty feet to my right. They were, it seemed, closing in. There was no time to be lost.

I took off in a flash through the maze of counters, and when I reached the street I zigzagged at full speed between the hundreds of pedestrians crowding the sidewalks. I was heading straight for the train station. My throat was dry and burning, my heart pounding wildly. I covered the mile or so in record time. I jumped on the last platform of the electric train, and went through a couple of compartments and huddled in a corner seat. A few seconds later the train left. My sprinting capability had really helped me!

Back in Antwerp thirty minutes later, I still ran the risk of possible search at the station. But luckily, the coast was clear.

Instead of going straight back to the hideout, I decided to make a detour. I had a dual purpose for this. I wanted to make a stop at a bookstore owned by a widow whose husband had been executed by the Germans for his Resistance activities quite early in the war.

But Yvonne Rahier, the bookstore owner, was also part of the Escape Line network. Maybe she could give me some better news about possible escape routes and hopes for movement again.

There were several customers in the store, so, after furtively acknowledging me, Yvonne continued taking care of them, and I perused the shelves, keeping an eye on her to take advantage of the first moment she would be free. This happened a few moments later. We could barely exchange a few words—guarded ones, of course. But, unfortunately, she didn't give me any hopeful signs.

As I was about to walk out, who should come into the store but Donald, the escort. He was understandably surprised to see me. I hadn't seen him since the day we were under siege in my apartment, the day he took his three men out.

His first question was, "Where have you been?" Then, "Where are you living now?" My answer, which he should have expected, was, "Sorry, I can't tell you that," and, bidding him a hurried goodbye, I stormed out of the bookstore.

I had to make quite sure now that Donald didn't trail me, so I took the usual precautions: speeding up, slowing down, turning back to a storefront, and thus retracing a few steps; making slight detours instead of going toward my hideout in a beeline. When quite assured I was alone, I hurried straight toward home.

My "fly boys" were disappointed when I told them about the failure in securing a linkage in Brussels. The complete blockage of the Escape Line was demoralizing.

The days seemed to linger on; the only excitement was the occasional evening visit of my fellow Resistance fighters. They brought news from the outside, and built up our hopes. There were some signs of possible movement.

Then finally, on July 10, came the good news: the five airmen would be picked up the following day, and would be on their way!

We all retired that evening with mixed feelings. We were relieved that the Escape Line was open, but we all had apprehension weighing heavily in our thoughts.

Morning came, and the hours ticked by until afternoon, when one of the agents chosen to escort the men arrived. He gave his instructions: the men would walk to the corner of the street, turn left, and proceed about thirty feet further to the stop of streetcar number 8. They were given money for the fare. The escort, of course, would not show any relationship to them. They were to look for his signal when to get off the streetcar.

The goodbyes were quite emotional. I tried not to show my feelings, but we had been together much longer than with any of the previous airmen. Gurth Webster and Len Collins had endured the anxiety of the siege around my apartment and the flight here to the hideout, and a bond of friendship had certainly been established. It hurt to see them go, but on the other hand, I was glad for them that they had another chance to return to England.

From behind the curtains of the front room I watched them walk away. A few minutes later the rumble of the streetcar filled the air; as it passed, I saw my "boys" standing on the platform. They were the last airmen I would have a chance to shelter.

I had a burning desire to get out of this house and back to my own apartment; but, of course, this would have been folly. So, as expected, my orders were to stay put until further notice.

One afternoon François came with the British agent I had met before on at least two occasions, the same who had asked me to keep his gun for him between meetings. I will call him Agent X. It was a real joy to see him again.

The visit seemed too short. I hated to see them go. I extended the pleasure of their company by walking with them to the crossroad, about a block away. It felt wonderful to be in the open air. This was the last time I would see Agent X.

Fortunately—as I considered it then—the orders to stay put were rescinded a couple of weeks later. I was told that one of our agents was working at the SS headquarters; therefore, if there were any imminent danger of arrest, our agent would know about it, and I would be notified.

So, with a big sigh of relief, I headed for home. How good I felt! I realized what a heavy load the airmen must have also shed upon leaving our hideout.

I had only been at home for a few hours when the dreaded doorbell rang. I couldn't believe my eyes when I opened the door.

There stood our big boss of Group G, Mr. De Beukelaer, who had come from Brussels to see me. He had been awarded the Silver Star after World War I, for his intelligence work. Now, in World War II, he was more active than ever, once again with the Resistance.

Mr. De Beukelaer was a big contractor, but had stopped all business activities because he did not want to work for the Germans. They had summoned him, demanding his cooperation, but he claimed he didn't have the needed materials or tools, and thus couldn't do the jobs for them. He refused steadfastly to work for the occupier, using every possible pretext. Of course, that meant he could not do work for anyone else; nevertheless, his trucks were used during the occupation to transport the drums of sabotage materiel from England.

His brother, also in the building trade I think, owned the warehouse in Malines where our Group G had its main depot.

Mr. De Beukelaer explained that my usefulness to the Resistance in Antwerp had been ruined by my having been marked by the enemy. Therefore he wanted me to work at the drop sites, where I would be the contact with the pilots of the drop plane. I was elated! He said he wanted me to leave now with him to go to Brussels.

I wanted to take care of a couple of errands the following morning, and suggested I join him in Brussels the next day. He agreed, and left.

I felt very tired that evening. Emotions had run high. I went to bed and slept like a log.

William Lynch

Part Four:
Arrest and Liberation

1 I woke up refreshed. Excited about the prospect of a new duty, I set out on my bicycle to take care of those couple of errands. It felt so good to move about again, instead of being cooped up as I had been for several weeks at the hideout. However, I went about my chores diligently, anxious to get back to my apartment, pick up my things, and leave for Brussels and my new assignment.

Back at the apartment, I left my bicycle on its stand in the hall downstairs and ran up the two flights of stairs two steps at a time. I closed the door to my apartment, crossed the little entrance hall, and deposited my handbag on the kitchen table about five steps from the entrance door. And there was a knock at the door.

There stood a civilian, rather short in stature. He asked me if I was "Madame Yvonne," which was how I was known to all contacts. I said yes. He slammed handcuffs on my left wrist (I was holding the door with that hand), and said, *"Deutsche Polizei!"* (German Police), then pushed the door open and slapped the other handcuff on my right wrist.

For a few moments my heart pounded wildly. This was the moment I had conditioned myself for ever since joining the Resistance. But despite this, the spontaneous human emotion gripped me on impact. This, I knew, was the end. I had been caught, and there was no way out.

After a couple of minutes I conquered my emotions, my heartbeat returned to its normal rhythm, and with it my calm composure returned. I was ready to face the inevitable.

The individual pushed me aside and entered the living room, heading straight for my telephone. He proceeded to take it apart, unscrewing the earpiece—which could be a good hiding place for messages, codes, etc. But he came up empty-handed! I suppressed a smile, and the first strong desire to challenge them face to face welled up in me.

I did, however, have some concerns. I still had some explosives in the apartment—not much, but some sticks of PE2, for instance, and a few other items. They were hidden in most casual places. One of these was the closet where my pails, mops, and cleaning utensils were stored. There was nothing I could do about this now—so why worry?

The first individual was shortly joined by a second, and about half an hour later, their search of the dining room buffet drawers was interrupted by the arrival of another agent, who seemed to be their superior.

The latter was a tall, slender man, impeccably dressed, and looking like a fashion plate. He stopped in front of me, looked me over, and with a big smile said: *"Ach, so das ist Madame Yvonne!"* (Well, so *that* is Madame Yvonne!)

After a few minutes of giving orders to his subordinates, he came back to me, and told me he was taking me away. He allowed me to go to the back of the apartment, where the bedroom and bathroom were located, to pick up my toothbrush, but he was right at my heels, of course. I wasn't permitted to take anything else.

One of the Germans preceded me down the stairs. He didn't leave the apartment empty-handed; he was carrying my portable type-writer. As we crossed the little hall on the ground floor and opened the front door, an order was barked from behind for him to also take my bicycle, which was standing in the hall.

In front of the house stood a panel truck. One of the men opened the back door of the vehicle and ordered me in. It already had two occupants: one of them was Mme. V, the owner of the hideout; the other, a male, was obviously another German agent, or a Belgian traitor working for the enemy. Mrs. V. started to say something, and was immediately told in no uncertain terms to shut up.

The panel truck moved away from the curb and off to . . . where? I had no idea to what branch of the German forces my captors belonged. The Gestapo or the SS? I would soon find out!

The van moved at a good clip, and I tried as best I could to get a glimpse of our route through the little back window of the truck. My fears grew and were confirmed when the driver took a turn near Avenue Prince Albert. I had very little doubt now as to what our destination was. A couple of minutes later, the panel truck went through the gate, and drove onto the grounds of a beautiful mansion which had been requisitioned by the German occupation forces and was now the dreaded SS headquarters. It was nicknamed "The Torture House" because of the horrors that took place there during interrogations.

We were ordered out of the truck, and led through the courtyard into the mansion. Mrs. V. tried again to address me upon leaving the truck, and was again harshly reminded by the guard to shut up. As we entered the mansion through the service entrance, she again tried to make a comment. At this point, the German agent grabbed her by the hair, and swung her across the hall to the base of the stairs. This obviously didn't deter her, because as we were climbing the stairs she tried again, which prompted me to hush her. It was most important not to show any relationship, any connection, and to avoid any recognition of one another!

We arrived in the attic; apparently, it must have been the servants' quarters at one time. Several doors gave out onto this level. I was pointed toward a spot near a wall, and ordered to face the wall. There was a lot of coming and going in and out of those rooms, and there were also several individuals just standing around. I felt as though hundreds of eyes were focused on me; a furtive look sideways confirmed the surveillance.

To keep up a pretense of nonchalance, I opened my handbag, retrieved my powder puff and lipstick, and acted as though I had no other worry than to improve my makeup. This prompted a very noticeable reaction from two of the SS agents standing close by.

This waiting period didn't help! I would certainly have preferred to know what lay ahead, bad though it certainly was going to be!

Finally, after what I guessed to be about half an hour, I was summoned to one of the rooms. A civilian was seated behind a desk to the left as I entered. I was greeted, once again, with, *"So, das ist Madame Yvonne!"* It started to have a very ominous sound!

Then came the paternal tone, and the admonition that it would be to my advantage to collaborate; it would make it so much easier. So why not tell him everything?

I put on my most innocent expression, and said, "Tell what? About what?"

"Whom did you work with? How many were involved? Who are they?" he asked.

"I don't know what you're talking about," was my answer.

The same questions were repeated over and over, then suddenly I was ushered out and back to the attic landing, and told to face the wall.

About fifteen minutes later I was called back in, and subjected to the same series of questions, to which my interrogator received the same answer, "I don't know what you are talking about." The only thing that was different in this exchange was the tone of my interrogator's voice. He had become more aggressive, more threatening.

Back out I went, with my face to the wall.

On the third return, my interrogator's gentlemanly behavior had vanished completely. The real SS tone—harsh and brutal—was now all too prominent!

As I stood in front of his desk, he at first repeated the same questions, and, as before received the identical naïve answer, "I don't know what you are talking about!" Then suddenly, he leaned forward, and slamming his fist on the desk, shouted, "If you act like a man, we will treat you like a man!"

Instead of intimidating me, this threat hardened my determination not to give in one bit. My interrogator rose, placed himself in front of me, and, accentuating his words with threatening gestures, shouted the same menacing words.

I maintained a blank expression, but I must admit that my heart was pounding wildly. Once again I was thrown out.

What would be the next episode? I didn't have to wait very long to find out. About ten minutes later I was sent back in. I was not alone with the agent in the room this time. About ten feet from the desk, with her back toward us, stood Mrs. V.

My interrogator asked me the same series of questions again, and received the same answer. Then, obviously upon an arranged signal, Mrs. V. turned around to face me and said in a clear, determined voice: "Ah, Yvonne! Why don't you tell them! They know everything, anyhow!"

I could have killed her! And if my eyes had been pistols she would have been dead right there and then. I stared at her, and with hatred in my voice I slowly said, marking each syllable, "And I don't know what *you* are talking about!"

There was silence in the room. My interrogator stared at me, then lifted the receiver of the telephone, and barked an order. A few minutes later the door opened, and in came two of his goons flanking the monk who had visited the airmen once in the hideout. My heart sank.

The monk presented a pitiful picture. Perspiration was running off his face. He seemed crushed. What had they done to him? He, who had had such a jolly disposition, who had given such help and moral support to so many of the Allied airmen he clandestinely escorted to safe havens.

My interrogator pointed toward Mrs. V. and asked slowly, "Do you know her?" The monk hesitated, then murmured: "I don't think so. . . ." The SS agent then pointed to me, and asked him the same question. The monk gave me a furtive glance, then answered, "That is Madame Yvonne."

I was dumbfounded; I felt betrayed. I certainly hadn't expected such behavior from him. I didn't let on, of course, and retained my appearance of cool composure.

My interrogator ordered the guards and their prisoner out, and Mrs. V. as well.

After the liberation of Antwerp, I ran into the monk at a ceremony. Obviously he felt he owed me an explanation and volunteered, "You have no idea what they did to me. They had dragged me up the stairs that day, pulling me by the hair!"

As they were leaving, another individual came in, tall, solidly built. The newcomer started an animated exchange with my interrogator. The din of their voices rose, giving me an opportunity to follow the discussion, which had become quite vehement. They were fighting over me, and who should have custody of me.

The discussion heated up quite considerably. I had no way of knowing who the new individual was or to what organization he belonged, for he was wearing civilian clothes. But anyone would be preferable to the one in whose custody I was at present: the dreaded SS! So, I silently rooted for the newcomer!

Suddenly, as their voices had reached quite a high pitch, the newcomer, accentuating each syllable, stated, "She is a military case, and is ours!" The SS agent, throwing a sheaf of papers on top of his desk, shouted back, "Take her away!"

Thereupon the newcomer turned to me and ordered me to follow him.

I felt relieved, although I still had no idea as to the affiliation of my new jailer! He certainly didn't lose any time, but took me at a fast clip down the two or three flights of steps and to his car.

I was ordered into the back seat: the agent sat next to me, and as the chauffeur drove off, my new custodian started a conversation—very civil, in a friendly tone of voice . . . too friendly. The caution flag rose up in me, and my answers were mainly monosyllabic replies.

We drove along the Chaussée de Malines, passing the Banque Nationale to the right. It became clear now where we were headed: the prison of Antwerp. A couple of minutes later the car entered the narrow Rue des Beguines, drove along the high red brick wall, and stopped in front of the big iron gate.

With a Machiavellian smile, my escort announced that here was where I would be staying. Instead of showing fear—which he obviously intended to instill in me—I smiled, and with a detached air I replied, "Oh! I have been here many times before!" I enjoyed his puzzled reaction, but the gate opened at that moment and we walked inside.

I had told him the truth. I had been inside the prison walls more than once; but not as a prisoner! My father's uncle had been director of the prison for several years, and as a child I had come with my father to dinner on Sundays. I remember how intrigued and impressed I was as a little girl to look up from the director's quarters at the solemn high walls with their small barred windows of the cells.

Tonight, however, as I walked through the big iron gate, instead of the director's entrance, things were quite different. It is difficult to describe what I felt at this time. Apprehension? Definitely. Fear? No doubt; how else could it have been? I knew what the end would be; I had always known, from the moment I joined the Resistance: if caught, there was no way out—the firing squad would be the end. But it was that which was to come in the meantime that was to be feared.

I was ushered into an office where a German in uniform took my personal belongings—money, watch, identity papers, etc. He was a young man; in his early thirties, maybe. He was very polite, even considerate. Detecting these traits, I risked addressing him, and proffered a request: "Would it be possible to notify someone—my uncle—that I am here?"

We were not alone in the office; there was another colleague of his at a desk a short distance away. He glanced in the direction of this colleague, then just above a whisper he said, "I am sorry, but that is forbidden." Looking at me he repeated quietly, "I am sorry, but that would be impossible!" The tone of voice, his gaze at me, his whole behavior convinced me that although this man wore the Nazi uniform, he did not do so of his free will. It practically boosted my morale!

The formalities accomplished, I was escorted back into the hall, and then through what seemed an endless number of locked doors. Then, entering a wing to the right, I was turned over to a German matron.

The Germans had taken over a part of the Antwerp prison for their Belgian political prisoners; I was now entering the women's wing. It was a long cell block two stories high, lined with solid doors with peepholes for each cell.

I was ordered up a spiral staircase to the second floor, then marched to the end of the catwalk.

The matron unlocked the door of the last cell, and ordered me in. The heavy door closed behind me. This was apparently a cell used for storage, and several mattresses were piled up against one wall almost to the ceiling.

I had no idea what time it was. The cell was dark, but a bright full moon shone right through the high, barred window, bathing one side of the cell in an eerie light.

It had been a day full of tension and anxiety, and a lot of unknowns lay still ahead. I felt empty and worn out.

I slipped my foot between the second and third lower mattresses, climbed up and grabbed the top one and pulled it toward me. After two or three attempts I succeeded in bringing it down. I placed it next to the pile, right in the middle of the cell, and stretched out, bathed in moonlight, wondering what was to come tomorrow.

2 Dawn came quickly, it seemed. I had been fortunate to fall asleep after what seemed like hours of going over the events of the day and wondering about the days ahead.

There seemed to be a lot of activity in the hall outside my cell. I could hear people shuffling back and forth and cell doors being opened and shut. No one opened mine until what seemed a couple of hours later.

I was marched downstairs and turned over to the same agent who had taken me away from the SS headquarters and brought me here the evening before. He now took me out of the prison and into a car parked near the entrance gate.

It was a beautiful sunny day. We left the narrow Rue des Beguines (Begynenstraat in Flemish), and, passing the Banque Nationale again, drove along the city park, past the Saint Joseph Church, and turned into the Avenue Charlotte. During the drive from the prison my escort, who was to become my regular interrogator, had been very civil, talking in a subdued tone, and giving me the expected advice that I should cooperate. I remained silent during the whole ride, except for polite monosyllabic acknowledgments. I was still at a loss as to where I was being taken and in whose custody I was, but my questions were answered when the driver turned left on the Avenue de Belgique and entered the driveway to the headquarters of the *Geheime Feldpolizei* (Secret Field Police). This headquarters had been established in a huge private property which, like so many others, had been requisitioned by the Germans.

The driveway extended right inside the building; the driver drove in and stopped the car next to a stone stairway to our left. I was ordered up the five or six steps, then through a double door and up another wide stairway to the second floor.

At the top of the stairs I was taken into a small office. It had a huge desk which faced the window and took up most of the space. There were two chairs, one facing the center of the desk, the other to its right, squeezed in between the right-hand side of the desk and the wall. I was ordered to sit there. A small cupboard with two doors stood against the wall to the right as one came in.

(Very soon I discovered the name of my interrogator. It was Helmer, and from here on I will refer to him by his name.)

Helmer sat down at the desk, and repeated his tirade about how much better and easier it would be for me to cooperate and tell him "everything." My answer, just as at the SS headquarters was, "I don't know what you are talking about!"

He stared at me, then picked up a package of cigarettes to his left and offered me one. I declined. He deposited the package on the desk, and in the same instant his right arm swung out and his hand hit the left side of my face with full force. My head bounced against the wall.

This was my initiation to Helmer's interrogation method!

During the next two hours, questions were thrown at me, interspersed with threats of harm that would certainly come my way if I didn't cooperate. My attitude remained unchanged: I feigned innocence and bewilderment at all these strange questions. Still, I must admit I had very little confidence I would convince my tormentor, no matter how good a facade I put up.

During these first two hours Helmer left the office several times for a few short moments each time. After a while I wondered what this tactic represented. Was this to try to throw me off balance by switching between the tension of incessant questioning to the relief of his absence, only to reappear and restart the verbal harassment? At regular intervals, his voice rose with exasperation until he again took a swing at me and his heavy hand landed with full force on the side of my face. Every time my head was sent bouncing against the wall. As a result, I soon lost the hearing in one ear, a condition which persisted for several days. I assume the eardrum, had sustained some kind of damage from the repeated hard impacts.

At about noon Helmer marched me out of his office and ordered me into another room, where as far as I can recall, the only furniture was a long table which occupied almost the whole length of the room, and a couple of chairs. I was left there.

It was a nice interlude. It was very quiet; there wasn't a voice nor even a step to break the silence.

The morning session had just been a foretaste of what was to come. There was no doubt in my mind that I was in for some rough times.

Helmer stayed away for what seemed a couple of hours. When he returned he had a totally different appearance. In the morning, when he fetched me at the prison, he had been wearing civilian clothes; now he was dressed in the green uniform of a German Gestapo officer. He looked like a different person. These changes of dress would become regular events in the days that followed. Helmer would change from civilian to a variety of military uniforms; sometimes he would even change from one civilian suit in the morning to another in the afternoon.

The afternoon session was a repetition of the morning session, and Helmer's exasperation grew with my continued statements of innocence. Finally, as the afternoon came to an end, he drove me back to the prison.

I was turned over to the German matron in the solitary confinement wing, and she marched me up the stairs as on the evening before, but stopped halfway down the row of cells, and unlocked a heavy door. I stepped inside Cell 260, which was to become my permanent "home."

In my cell stood a small table with a metal grill on two sides and a bottom shelf. On this shelf lay a straw mattress folded in two and a blanket. It didn't take a genius to figure out that this table was to become my bed for the night by tilting the table top completely sideways. A chair stood at one end of the table. Near the door, to the left as one entered, was a little shelf on which stood a pitcher of water and a small bowl for a wash basin; a pail which was to serve as toilet stood on the ground. If I remember correctly, there was a little corner shelf on the other side of the door as well. The floor was tiled; a small barred window was high in the wall opposite the cell door. It had little panes of heavy glass. A heavy pipe stretched across the wall below the window, a foot or so above the floor. It was obviously a heating pipe, and ran the whole length of the building.

The first thought that came to my mind was the need to keep track of the days. I sat down at my table and studied the white-washed walls, looking for a place where I could scratch a calendar without its being detected. I scanned the walls, imagining the matron entering my cell, and carefully chose one spot on the wall. My strong, hard fingernails came in handy, and in no time I had my calendar established. Now, each day I had only to scratch across one square, and I would not lose track of time.

I felt quite tired. Night had fallen, and the moonlight again threw light into my cell, but not in a straight line like the night before. I managed the transformation of my table into a bed; I unfolded the straw mattress and the blanket, and, after removing my dress, stretched out. I had no night clothes; I had not been allowed to take anything but my toothbrush with me when I was arrested.

I thought I would be able to fall asleep without delay because of my mental fatigue. Unfortunately, this was not the case. Once again, the events of the day kept going through my mind.

Then I felt a bite. Mosquitoes always love to use me as their target. A few moments later there came another attack. But why didn't I hear their usual drone? When a third attack came, despite a tremendous revulsion I have for squashing insects, I couldn't stand it anymore, and landed my hand on my face where I knew the culprit was. To my horror, I hit something much bigger than a mosquito! I felt panicky, but in my panic suddenly realized who my enemies were: bedbugs!

From that moment on, the war was on. Instead of resting and building up some strength for the day ahead, I spent a practically sleepless night fighting the creatures in the dark. They, however, scored many hits. They fed on my blood, and left their mark. By morning, in addition to the damage caused by Helmer's hand, my nocturnal foes had left me with a rather puffy appearance.

I was roused by a banging on my cell door and the loudly shouted order: *"Aufstehen! Aufstehen!"* (Get up! Get up!)

The aluminum washbowl was not much bigger than an American GI helmet; but I managed to make my ablutions.

There seemed to be a lot of activity going on in the building; lots of running back and forth. Very soon I learned the cause.

The cell door opened, and the matron stood at the entrance with another female prisoner. I was ordered to hand over my toilet pail, which the prisoner picked up. A couple of minutes later the door opened again, and a pail of water and a cleaning rag were handed to me. I was instructed to swab the cell floor, and *schnell* (fast). This became a daily routine.

About ten minutes later, the pail with the dirty water was retrieved. As soon as the door was locked again, I climbed on the pipe below the barred window, and pulled myself up to try to have a view of the outside world. I had tried the night before upon my return from interrogation, but it already had been too dark to really distinguish my surroundings.

A little corner of the inner courtyard and what I seemed to recognize as a corner of the director's quarters' garden was visible.

Shortly, I heard what was already becoming a familiar sound—the key turning in the keyhole—and an aluminum cup with boiling hot ersatz coffee, and a slice of bread with a piece of butter were placed on the floor at the entrance of my cell.

I proceeded to mark my butter with little lines at regular intervals so as to ration it for a week! I abandoned this method the following week, and instead used as much as necessary to at least taste the butter, and ate the bread dry for the rest of the week.

It is peculiar how solitude sharpens the senses. One's hearing seems to pick up every little noise. I soon learned to recognize the daily call from the ground floor of my wing that signaled my departure for interrogation at the Geheime Feldpolizei headquarters. Today, however, was the first time I heard it, and I didn't yet realize what it was; but when a day or two later, I learned that I had a prisoner number, the words fell into place. From then on, the order, *"Zwei und Dreizig Dreizehn Haus Heraus"* (3213 out of the house) was a dreaded one.

A few moments later the key turned in the keyhole and the matron ordered me out. She led me along the catwalk, down the little corkscrew staircase, across the hall, and through the group of locked doors, and I found myself back in Helmer's hands.

The drive back to the Geheime Feldpolizei headquarters was then—and every day after that—a kind of respite despite the physical abuse I would face and the mental tension and the constant fear of the unknown in the following hours. But to drive along, to see the park, the trees, even the possibility of a glimpse of a friend, made me feel alive during that short ride.

One morning as we were driving along the Avenue de Belgique close to the headquarters, I thought I saw someone I knew, and turned slightly to check the license plate of his car. This didn't escape Helmer, and with a cynical grin he inquired if that were a friend. Very coldly and calmly I told him "No such luck!" which was a lie. I had seen the car of a dear friend, the family doctor.

Back in Helmer's office, I was assigned to the same chair, squeezed in the same narrow spot, and greeted with the same offering: *"Eine zigarette, Yvonne?"* in his charming tone of voice, followed by the instantaneous transformation into the brutal, sadistic inquisitor.

My head bounced a few more times against the wall that day.

Helmer's questioning was at first directed mainly at the sheltering of downed Allied airmen. "Where did they come from? Where had they been before coming to you? Where did they go after leaving you? Who brought them to you?" and so on. To each and every question I proclaimed that I didn't have the slightest idea what he was talking about. This enraged Helmer.

At noon that day I was once again transferred to another room and Helmer disappeared, but not for long. He returned about fifteen minutes later, accompanied by another man in civilian clothes who, to judge by Helmer's respectful comportment toward him and by the visitor's own manner, seemed to be a high-ranking superior.

I was seated a short distance from a long table. They walked along the other side of the table and stopped opposite me. There, Helmer, with a Draculian smile, said, *"Das ist Madame Yvonne,"* to which the visitor responded: *"Ach, so das ist Yvonne!"* And Helmer added, *"Eine sehr gefährliche Frau."* (very dangerous woman.)

Maybe I should have felt proud to have such a reputation among such company!

The rest of the day showed clearly that Helmer's patience was running out. His demeanor became rougher by the minute. Toward the end of the day, he announced he was going to check my apartment. "I am sure I will find some interesting things," he said with a sinister grin. In turn, I retorted with a cocky, "I wouldn't know what!" Another lie! I *knew* I had one explosive charge hidden in the kitchen closet among the brushes and pails. It was one left from an aborted mission.

3 Next morning we rode in total silence from the prison to the Geheime Feldpolizei headquarters. The air was heavy. Back in Helmer's office, I was seated in my same corner, but there was no *"Eine zigarette, Yvonne?"* this morning. Instead, Helmer's facial expression was hard and stern. He remained silent until he sat to my left, at his desk. Then he picked up something he had hidden to the left of his typewriter, out of my sight, and slammed it on top of his desk in front of me. *"Und was ist das?"* (And what is that?) he shouted. It was two sticks of PE2, the putty-like explosives parachuted to us from England.

Keeping an expression of total ignorance, and lifting my shoulders to emphasize my reply, I said, *"Das weiss ich nicht!"* (I don't know!)

In a rage, Helmer shouted back, *"Das ist Springstoff!"* (Those are explosives!) I put on a show of fear, cringing back in my chair as far away from the stuff as possible.

Helmer was beside himself. He raved, threatened, and relentlessly shouted questions at me as to the origin of the explosives, the individuals involved in supplying it, and where it had been used.

"Where did it come from?" That question needed an answer, and an answer which would eliminate involving the use.

I suspected that I had been under surveillance for quite a while, obviously even before the betrayal the day I had the five Allied airmen in my home. Therefore, they had certainly witnessed the coming and going of men to my home. They might even have witnessed the delivery or pickup of the big package containing the transmitter.

Thus I concocted the following scenario:

These two sticks, which I thought were putty, had fallen out of a big parcel left with me by an individual whom I had casually met. This individual and I had been discussing, during a streetcar ride, the food shortages, and how lucky one was to have a source of black market food items available. I said this man had asked me if I would be willing from time to time to accept a bundle delivered by him or someone else, to be picked up a couple of days later. I said to Helmer: "We have to eat, you know! I was glad to help this man if I could!"

I continued: "These two packages of putty had fallen out of the last bundle of groceries I accepted, and I only saw them on the floor of my den next to the sofa where I had kept the bundle, the day after it was taken away. I put them in my kitchen closet with the cleaning materials. (I knew that was where Helmer had found them.) Not having received another delivery, I hadn't been able to return them to their rightful owner.

A very plausible story, I thought, and I stuck to it!

Now came the description of this apocryphal friend. In order not to falter during subsequent interrogations on the subject, I chose a cousin of my husband's who I knew was far away out of reach on another continent and described him as the man who had left the "groceries."

It was a relief to be back in my solitary cell that night. I had a lot to think about. More than ever, I was in for some in-depth grilling.

From now on, all questions would be related to the sabotage materials. One morning, with a sarcastic smile, Helmer placed in front of me a package of four-by-five cards with names of the Allied airmen I had sheltered. I remember the top card bore the name of Charles Shierlaw from Canada.

"You see, we know it all," he said.

From then on, my interrogation was handled by Helmer and two of his acolytes. The rough treatment really started now. The slapping was upgraded to whipping.

One of the acolytes was a short little guy with a mouse-like expression. His first interest was in the direction taken by the supposed individual who had picked up the supposed parcels. He had a map.

I told him I didn't pay any attention to where the man was going. I said, "I handed him the bundle at the front door. It was dark. He left through the little front garden, and I think I saw him go to the right." (This was in the direction of the park, where the acres of wide open space afforded lots of opportunity to disappear.)

For hours on end, this interrogator, the second agent, and Helmer threw questions at me in fast succession—a typical "grilling" designed to induce "slips" on the part of the accused.

After a couple more days of these tactics, I was marched down to an office on the ground floor. A guard stood at the door; it was, no doubt, the office of the commandant.

The door opened, and I found myself about thirty feet away from a big desk set in the far corner of what was once probably the big living room of this apartment. Behind the desk sat an officer; I seem to remember he was a colonel.

In the most civil manner, the colonel invited me to sit opposite him at the desk. He treated me most courteously. His mannerism, his speech, everything was of the finest quality.

This was not, however, making me feel comfortable. To the contrary, I was more than ever on my guard. He spoke once again, like the others, about the advantage of cooperation, and encouraged me to tell them all. The admonition lasted quite a while, and it was all in the same kind, respectful tone. When he was through, I responded the way I had for days, "I don't know; I can't give you any information; I don't know anything," etc.

His reaction was instantaneous, and this gentleman officer was transformed into a vicious, cruel agent of the secret service. He snapped back at me like a mad dog, then called the guard, with the order, "Take her away; you know what you have to do!"

That was an ominous threat!

There was another type of interlude the following day. It had been a rough morning, with questions thrown at me by all three interrogators, interspersed with threats and blows. When their lunchtime came I was marched into an enormous front room that looked like a small ballroom. A German corporal was my guard.

There were no chairs, so I stood near the windows. After a short while, the guard walked over to me, and in no time he tried to fondle me. I was physically strong, having been a gymnast for years, and was successful in foiling his attempt. However, I will never forget the sight of this young man in his green-gray uniform having an orgasm while standing two feet from me!

During another of their lunch hours, I was locked up in a small bathroom. I had the choice of sitting on the toilet or the bidet, or crawling into the bathtub!

After a while I had a visitor, who was a welcome sight. I never knew his name, but he was a gentleman. He had his office adjacent to Helmer's; during the first days, when I was being grilled by Helmer in his office, I could see this man through the window, interrogating his prisoners. There was never any violence on his part, nor, it seemed, any shouting.

One early evening, when Helmer was still badgering me, this man had walked in and suggested to Helmer that he let him take me back to the prison. Helmer was raving mad at me; at first he rejected the offer, saying he wasn't through with me. But his colleague insisted that it was late—it was about 6:45 P.M. by then—and Helmer finally agreed to let me go.

All during the ride to the Rue des Beguines, he spoke in soft tones, expressing regrets for the rough treatment to which I had been subjected. It would help if I would cooperate, he added. No matter if he, too, was only trying to make me talk; his kindness and warmth were a welcome relief!

Now, today, in these most unusual surroundings, he once again had a few soothing words!

A bag had been delivered to me in prison; a big pillowcase with my name and number stitched in red embroidery thread on it: "3213 Yvonne Judels—de Ridder." It contained a nice cotton dress, a change of underwear, and some small scissors with rounded ends. It was a wonderfully welcome present. I had been living for days in the same clothes I was wearing when arrested.

The scissors were also a more than welcome item. I had really started worrying about having my toenails grow back into my feet! Having curled-down toes, this seemed a possibility!

I should insert here that these welcome items were provided by an aunt, my father's brother's wife. We had been estranged for years because of a family feud. I had always felt a great love for my uncle, but had seen him less than half a dozen times in twenty years! In the last few months, however, since I had broken off from my parental home, I had had the joy of seeing him and his wife again.

How did it happen that *she* provided me this so welcome package? She had gone to my father's home and asked my stepmother if Viviane, my half-sister, would provide a change of clothes for me. Viviane was called, and when presented with the request answered, "I have nothing to give!" (What a vivid picture of the fiend that girl was!) My aunt was shocked, so she had *her* daughter—my cousin—make the gift of one of her dresses and pieces of underwear.

The dreaded *"3213 Haus heraus"* echoed down the hall. Soon the muted steps of one of the German matrons sounded close by and the door opened.

This was to be one of the worst days at the Geheime Feldpolizei headquarters. The atmosphere seemed "charged"; my three interrogators appeared ready for the kill. First the same series of questions were thrown at me in fast succession by one, then another of the agents, with the usual tactics used to throw me off guard. I hadn't fallen into that trap, and this seemed to drive them up the wall!

Suddenly, Helmer pulled a footlocker-like container from against the wall to the center of the room, and placed it next to me. He flipped it open, and screamed at me: *"Und was ist das?"* (And what is that?)

Again I had to master a totally blank expression and feign ignorance. But there in the footlocker were samples of virtually everything we used for sabotage. PE2, delay pencils, cords, capsules, etc., most of it probably recovered by the Germans when some of our men were caught, or when charges were discovered and disconnected.

My repeated declaration of ignorance seemed to unleash heretofore unseen degrees of fury in Helmer. He slammed the footlocker shut, and ordered me to "lie down" on top of it. I looked at him in amazed disbelief. Did he really expect me to lie down there and just wait to be beaten? My show of disdain released all bounds of fury in him. He ordered his two acolytes to put me down.

I repeat again, I was rather strong physically, and limber. They didn't succeed. Each held me by one arm, and they tried to get me down on the box. I wriggled, trying to keep my legs on each side of the box; they pushed and pulled while Helmer whipped me mercilessly with a long leather cane like a riding crop, only twice as long.

The blows fell hard, cutting like fire; my legs were also being torn apart. I had almost no skin left on either shin from the scraping on the box's edge as they fought to put me down.

All the while I kept yelling at the top of my voice, "I don't know anything!" Finally Helmer screamed back at me, "Be quiet," and he continued his relentless beating.

Finally I went limp and collapsed to the ground, rolling on my back and gasping for air. Helmer stood on top of me and, raising his arm, struck me across the front. Amazingly, this brought an outcry from his colleague. *"Sind Sie verückt?"* (Are you crazy?) he asked, and stopped Helmer's beatings.

When I went down gasping for air I thought it was the end. I thought I would be dead in the next few seconds.

Then I saw Helmer looking down at me, saying, "When you recover, we'll start again."

I slowly regained my breath and got back on my feet. Instead of the promised renewed flagellation, I was instead marched down two flights of stairs and into the cellar. My backside and the upper portion of my legs felt as though they were on fire, and seemed to weigh hundreds of pounds!

There were two uniformed Germans waiting in the cellar, flanked by two black-uniformed underlings. The cell I was ordered into was a wine cellar with its typical *caveaux* (vaulted niches) for storing wines. There were two wicker chairs—the tub-type so familiar a few years ago as patio furniture; one of them was normal size, the other a child's or doll's replica.

One of the Germans ordered me to sit down. *"Setzen Sie,"* he barked. I declined. *"Nein, Danke, Ich kann nicht sitzen!"* (No, thank you, I cannot sit!) He barked back his order to sit. I took my time, trying to find one little spot on my posterior which did not send unbearable pain through my system.

The four agents seemed to enjoy my exercise; they stood there silently following my every movement. When I finally sat still, the one in command said slowly and with a diabolical smile, *"Nein, nicht da!"* (No, not there!) and pointed to the diminutive replica of a chair.

I looked at him and got up slowly from my so laboriously conquered seat. I lifted my shoulders, a gesture to convey to him, "So what, if that's what you want, you'll have to wait much longer!" I was not about to show them they were getting to me.

When I had finally managed to squeeze part of my anatomy onto the edge of this Lilliputian piece of furniture, he turned and slammed the wooden slat door, and left with two of his acolytes. One black-uniformed individual was left to guard me.

As soon as the three were out of sight, and out of earshot, this black-shirt came close to my door, and addressed me in a very low voice. I couldn't hear what he was saying; he repeated it again, but because he was just speaking above a whisper, I was again unable to comprehend. But his manner of speech seemed quite unusual, so I gathered all my strength to get up from my seat, and took the two steps that separated me from the door.

He spoke in Flemish (from which I deduced he was a Belgian traitor) and said, "If you have to go to the girl's room, tell me now; very shortly I will be replaced, and *that* one won't let you go!"

I replied: "No, thank you, I have no need, they beat me dry!" and added, "You want to see?" Upon which I lifted my skirt, and showed him the lower part of my anatomy, which was totally mauve-black with deep wedges where the leather cane had repeatedly struck.

The guard struck his head literally against the slats of the door, and in a muffled voice, emphatically ordered me to report this to the prison doctor.

I was standing there holding onto the slats of the door when suddenly it seemed as if everything started to sway; a funny feeling came to the base of my skull, and I told my guard, "I think I am going to faint."

I had never fainted before in my life. I don't know how long I was out, but when I came to I found myself stretched out on the brick floor of the cellar, the door wide open, and the same agents who had played the sadistic game with the chairs stood there.

As I stirred, their superior spoke: *"Was ist los?"* (What's wrong?) I got back on my feet as best I could. It was obvious what was wrong. . . . I had passed out! "That's all," was his retort. "In a short while we'll get back to you." He waited until I was seated in the infant chair again, then left. The door slammed, and the footsteps echoed in the distance.

Now the terrible pain from the beatings was dwarfed by an unbearably excruciating headache. My head felt as it if were split right open two-thirds of the way toward the base of the skull!

What must have happened was that when I fainted I struck my head on the horizontal partition (the niche), and from that brick platform fell to the brick floor. The pain was unbearable; so blinding was it that it made the whipping wounds seem more endurable by contrast!

I was seated in my mini-chair, and swore I wouldn't move again until they came to get me. I didn't expect this wait to last for several hours. It was late afternoon when I was ordered out and marched back upstairs.

When I got up I wondered if I would be able to make a single step! For hours I had sat immobile, and the lower part of my body had been beaten to a pulp! My blood circulation had been seriously impaired for hours now. I felt as stiff as a board, and numb. But for nothing in the world would I give them any show of pain or handicap.

The guard led me out of the cellar, then back to the long wide staircase. Was I going to be able to feign normality here? I walked to the right edge of the staircase and, holding on firmly to the railing, I hoisted myself at every step while trying to appear as normal as possible.

When I was brought back to the big interrogation room Helmer wasn't in sight, and that was a relief. At the desk in the middle of the back wall sat Helmer's colleague, whose name I can't recall. He had always been stern, even hard, but never sadistic and cruel like Helmer.

I was ordered to stand in front of his desk. He proceeded to question me again on the same subject, and I continued to deny my knowledge of any of the sabotage materiel or activities.

Suddenly the agent slammed his fist on the desk, leaned forward toward me, and exclaimed, *"Eine Harte wie Sie habe ich nie gekannt!"* (A hard one like you I have never known!) I smiled, lifted my eyebrows in faked astonishment.

I was "dismissed" and escorted back to prison.

4   The pain was excruciating. The straw mattress on my cot did not help to soothe or cushion my injuries. There was no position which provided me any relief from physical agony. Every inch of my anatomy was raw. Although it was my backside which had been massacred, even when I tried to lie face down every muscle and nerve sent sharp shots through my system.

Dawn was welcome. I tried my best to combat the stiffness that had set in. The morning routines of swabbing the floor of my cell and eating my pittance kept my mind occupied, but then came the agonizing period of waiting for the dreaded call, "Out of the house." And this morning it was more dreadful than ever!

The minutes ticked by, but no call came. Mid-morning, a time when I was always at the Geheime Feldpolizei headquarters, was, I found out, exercise time at the prison. I could hear all the doors being opened one after the other. The key turned in my keyhole too, but, probably because I was always out by that hour, the matron did not really push the door open.

But I was not about to be confined there, if there were a possibility to be in the open air. The door was built in such a way that the wide jamb had a kind of suction effect against the thick wall. I pulled, literally clawed—it was the only way for me to have some hold on the door—and after what seemed an eternity I finally succeeded in opening it.

But now I found myself alone in a deserted wing. Not a soul was in sight, and I was a target for whichever of the guards might suddenly appear.

Nevertheless, I was determined to get outside and join the others. I carefully descended the little corkscrew staircase, and followed a path leading to the outside court.

The exercise court was triangular in shape, with a little two-foot red brick path winding between flowerbeds planted with low greenery. A matron stood at each of two of the points of the triangle; at the third one, near the door, stood the Feldwebel, the male sergeant. He barely gave me a sidelong glance as I fell in step behind another female prisoner.

We were to walk in single file at distance of five feet from one another, and to keep up a good pace, in silence! I quickly realized that in my present physical condition I would be unable to keep up the pace. I tried and tried to lengthen my gait, but to no avail. The distance between the prisoner ahead of me and myself increased. As I marched past the Feldwebel, he barked, *"Was ist los?"* (What's wrong?) I responded, *"Nichts"* (Nothing), and tried again to lengthen my step.

On the next pass in front of him, the Feldwebel repeated his inquiry, but in a much more pressing manner that demanded an answer. I responded that I had been beaten. "By whom?" he asked. "Geheime Feldpolizei," was my answer. He ordered me to walk back and forth in the little space behind him.

A few minutes later the exercise period came to an end, and we were all marched back to our cells. I was barely locked back in when the head matron appeared. She had impressed me as a strict disciplinarian, but a decent individual. She questioned me, asked me to show her the damage, and asked who had perpetrated it. She displayed genuine outrage, and stormed out.

A few minutes later another visitor arrived, a matron whom I despised. She was an underhanded, sneaky type, and had a specialty of walking around after dark, always with complete muffled footsteps. I had very acute hearing, however, and could always hear her approach. Then, very quietly, she would peek through the peephole in the door. One evening I heard her approach and hid behind the low little screen standing by the side of the pail. I enjoyed listening to her frantically looking left and right, but I finally decided the joke had lasted long enough, and I showed myself as I moved back toward my cot. I was tempted to wave to her, but I decided it was better not to antagonize her.

Now this despised individual entered my cell, and with a false tone of commiseration she asked, *"Was ist los, mein Kind?"* (What's wrong, my child?). I showed her the damage; she displayed disapproval, and left.

A little while later the head matron fetched me and told me she was taking me to see the doctor. And off I went with her through a series of locked doors.

I found myself in the doctor's waiting room. The matron left me there while she entered the doctor's office. In the waiting room were about ten women prisoners waiting to be examined. Among them was a very tall young woman whom I knew. She was the daughter of a well-to-do and well-known family in Antwerp. I wondered why she had been incarcerated. She was also a special prisoner for she seemed to be in a rather advanced stage of pregnancy.

To give a vivid example of the humiliation inflicted by the Nazi occupier, I witnessed this refined, well-bred young woman as she was obliged to submit to a most intimate medical examination by a German nurse, right there in front of all of us.

It turned out that my examination was not going to be public. Apparently they did not want the other prisoners to see the flagrant marks of the brutality to which I had been subjected. I was called out of the waiting room and ordered in the doctor's office.

The doctor was a German officer, of course; he was middle-aged, and very gentlemanly. He had me lean against a board or wall, then lifted my skirt and started poking gently all over the swollen and battered mauve-black surface of the lower part of my body. Every poke, no matter how gentle, was sheer agony. It almost hurt more than the sharp, hard blows of Helmer's whip!

The doctor commented on my condition to the chief matron and asked her who was responsible for it. "Geheime Feldpolizei" was her answer. Instantly the doctor grabbed the edge of my skirt and pulled it back down with the statement, *"Geheime Feldpolizei. Dann kann ich nichts machen!"* (Secret Field Police. . . . Then I can't do a thing!)

In other words, the Geheime Feldpolizei was almighty; no one could touch them. They were not to be challenged by anyone!

I was lucky that day. I was not taken out for interrogation. At least twenty-four hours of respite, and it was well needed!

The following morning I had no such luck! The call for my exit echoed from the lower level of the ward. Half an hour later I was back in Helmer's office, and he started the session with a new threat.

In his cold, cutting, venomous style he warned, "We will put you in a place where there is no pity and no doctor!" It seemed, nevertheless, that some report or some complaint had found its way from the prison to the Geheime Feldpolizei headquarters. Other threats followed. "We have other ways to make you talk, you know!" he yelled. How well did I know!

Except for the mental harassment by my three interrogators, no physical brutality was performed that day.

Back in my cell that evening, I was alerted by a tapping sound. The origin wasn't difficult to trace: it came from the heating pipe. The tapping was repeated, then I tapped back on the pipe with the identical rhythm. Then, putting my ear against the pipe, I could vaguely hear a muffled voice. In a soft voice I said, "I can't understand you." I was whispering into an interstice where the pipe entered the wall and an aluminum plate surrounded the pipe, closing the hole in the wall.

The voice on the other side said: "Move the plate, we will hear each other better." I hesitated, but what could I lose? The plate moved easily, and there was the voice of my neighbor coming through clearly.

I didn't think the adjacent cell had been occupied during the previous days. My neighbor asked me, "Why are you here?" I was on guard! "I don't know," I replied. She insisted, but I only gave the same answer, adding that they were accusing me of all sorts of things, and I didn't know what they were talking about! I asked what the reason was for her incarceration, and she gave me a vague answer. I have no doubt she was a plant.

The same thing happened the following night. This time my neighbor's questions convinced me more than ever that she was a German agent.

The following morning, as I was waiting to be taken out for interrogation, the Feldwebel, accompanied by a young matron, came in on inspection. This was a test. Would he discover my calendar, the one I had scratched in the white-washed wall the evening of my arrival in this cell? I had, it seemed, chosen my spot very well, for they didn't discover it!

When they came in I was seated at my table. They took about three steps inside the cell, then the Feldwebel sarcastically said, "She doesn't know, it seems, she is to stand below the window!" I literally jumped up from my chair, and made one big leap in my best gymnastic form, which landed me in the indicated spot. I whirled around, and stood at attention, military style, facing them. I brought a smile to his face.

The Feldwebel walked straight to the corner of the cell, and at the point where the pipe goes through the wall he slipped the piece of aluminum aside, exposing the hole. "Well, did we have some nice conversations?" he asked. I lifted my shoulders in response. Turning to the matron, he added: "Maybe we should eliminate forks and spoons, when serving the food!" (inferring these could be used to dig).

By the way, the plant was soon removed. The plot had not worked out!

As explained before, the prison wing in which I was held had been taken over by the Germans to hold their political prisoners. The ground floor was occupied by women prisoners—six or seven to a cell. On the second floor, where I was, were women held in solitary confinement. As far as I know, however, there was only one other woman prisoner on this floor, although there might have been a second. On the third floor, the male prisoners were held.

The floor of my cell was tiled, and one of those tiles was slightly loose. One of the first days of my occupancy, early in the morning, the German matron had come in with a civilian. He was a Belgian prisoner, non-political; he had probably been incarcerated for smuggling a sack of potatoes, or something of the kind. Prisoners like him it seemed, were used to perform some minor repairs around the prison wards.

She pointed out to him the loose tile, and he proceeded to work on it. After a few seconds, when the matron had moved slightly outside my cell, he whispered to me, "Why don't you break a window? You'll get more air!" My expression of puzzlement probably prompted him to add, "Haven't you heard the breakage at night?" I hadn't, but I kept his advice in mind, and managed to muffle the impact of the blow that same evening; because of my fear of being found out, I didn't use enough force on my first try, and it took me two or three efforts to shatter one of the small panes of thick glass between the bars. It was indeed an improvement!

The man gave me another piece of advice, again whispered during a few seconds of inattention on the part of the matron. "As soon as we leave, start stepping on the tile to loosen it up so I'll have to come back!" I did just that, and he *was* sent back a few days later. We exchanged conspirators' smiles when he entered my cell. He also indicated he noticed I had followed his advice regarding the window.

These little incidents were nothing in themselves, but they nevertheless represented such a welcome mental relief.

The little opening to the outside world made a big difference, both visually and audibly. I could see much more clearly the corner of the courtyard below; I could hear the chatter of birds much more distinctly, and even could put some crumbs of a couple of Red Cross cookies on the ledge. The cookies had come with my ration one day, but I didn't like them.

I could also hear distinctly the German guard in the courtyard ordering *"Ruhe!"* (silence), whenever the noise coming from the surrounding cells was, in his opinion, too loud.

One evening, back in my cell after a grueling interrogation session at the Geheime Feldpolizei headquarters I had climbed on the pipes and, holding on to the bars, lifted myself up, taking in big gulps of the evening air. Suddenly from the men's section above I heard a cough—a very special cough. My father's! No matter where, no matter how big a crowd we might be in, I could always recognize my father's cough. There was no mistake, that was his! My heart sank. Had he been arrested too?

I wondered how I could communicate with my father. I couldn't call out his name; the guard was there at all times. Suddenly I had a thought. On my mother's tomb, my father had inscribed two lines of a melody my mother, a musician, had in her repertory.

> Adieu, Rayons et Roses
> Adieu, Bonheur trop court
> (Goodbye rays and roses/
> Goodbye happiness too short)

He loved that song. If he heard it, there would immediately be a sign of recognition. I held on to the bars, and just loud enough to reach the floor above but not loud enough to be heard by the guard below, I sang the verses. No responses! I tried a second time, louder. Still, no response!

After the liberation I found out that my father was, indeed, in that cell, but with six other prisoners; conversations among the prisoners had prevented him from hearing my message!

5 My interrogation sessions came less regularly; it was sometimes mid-morning before I was picked up. Nevertheless, the questions of the three agents assigned to my case continued to be thrown at me incessantly.

I continued to plead ignorance of whatever they accused me of and I also hung onto the scenario I had concocted for part of the subjects I had to have an explanation for.

Helmer, obviously, had not found any additional incriminating evidence on his subsequent visits to my apartment, but I was both curious and apprehensive about a remark he made to me before one of his searches. In a rage he had told me, "I'll do to you what they have done to me!" What did he mean? Who were "they"? British? Americans? Did he live in England? In America? (He spoke English fluently.) Had they confiscated his belongings? Had someone in either country destroyed his belongings?

I wondered. If by any miracles I came out of this alive, would I find every possession gone, destroyed, or stolen? Well, this problem was being solved that day. There was no need to worry anymore!

Toward the end of the day I was brought to face my three tormentors. There I was notified by the one I assumed to be the senior ranking member of the group, that I had six weeks to go! In six weeks I would be executed!

This was no surprise to me. From the moment I joined the Resistance I had known that my activities would mean the death penalty if I were caught. Surely, the day I was arrested, this same thought became reality, and I never expected any other finale.

So, when the words were pronounced, when the sentence was stipulated, it didn't cause me any shock. I looked at them impassively, even with a smile at the corners of my mouth as if to say, "So what? I knew it all the time!"

Helmer read my mind. Leaning forward, he snarled: *"Sie werden nicht erschossen, Yvonne; hangen sollen Sie!"* (You will not be shot, Yvonne, you will be hanged!) This was a shock. I mastered keeping an impassive expression, but I felt as if all the blood had drained out of my veins!

(The punishment of hanging was indicated by my involvement in sabotage. I had been unaware that this was their rule!)

I was driven back to prison. I sat at my table, and for the first time I broke down. After a good cry, I got hold of myself and concentrated on visualizing the whole hanging procedure. I spent most of the night going over and over what I imagined the procedure to be, and by morning I was over my fear.

Although I had no news of the war, the wailing sirens announcing the approach of aircraft had been quite active in the last week; no doubt our side was flying over Belgium at a regular pace to pound the German forces on Belgian soil as well as those on German soil. It was a delight to hear the drone of the big Allied bombers. All this, it seemed, indicated the Allied forces were getting near.

When the sirens sounded, the German personnel came to put double-locks on our doors, then they all disappeared into the shelters. If a bomb hit the prison, we prisoners would be caught like rats, while they were safe!

One morning that week I was still in my cell at exercise time, and I was marched to the yard with the others. As we started our drill—walking five feet apart in silence—I noticed in the far corner building, about fifty feet from our serpentine path, three or four people, civilians, standing in an open window, watching us. This was an office in the Belgian wing of the prison.

On my second pass I recognized one of the men. He was "Uncle Henry," a friend of my father's who was a member of the Prison Commission. My heart welled up. I started making signals every time I faced that side: passing my hand over my hair, then lifting my arm before bringing it down in a big arc, etc. Did he recognize my efforts to signal? I will never know.

(After the liberation, I learned that that day someone in that office had pointed me out, saying, "That one has been condemned to death." The news had leaked out quickly to the Belgian Resistance!)

Something was afoot. This was the second evening that a big to-do had taken place on the ground floor. I could hear the cell doors being opened; women prisoners gathering in the hall, talking excitedly; an occasional yell from a woman. Were they setting prisoners free?

The following morning I was marched down to a small office on the prison grounds. Helmer was there in his gray-green uniform. Why was I being questioned here? I had no complaint about it, though; no brutality was allowed here! It was a short session, and soon I was marched back to my cell.

With darkness came the usual round-up of prisoners. I heard one of the solitary confinement cells being opened this time. Slowly silence enveloped our world again.

At daybreak the usual routine was followed by a surprise order. Shortly after I had swabbed the floor and turned over my pail of water to the prisoner on duty, the door opened again and there stood a young matron ordering, *"Schnell, alles einpacken!"* (Quickly, pack everything.)

"Alles einpacken!"—what a joke! My *"alles"* consisted of the clothes I had on my back, plus the old pillowcase containing a change of underwear and the dress in which I came to prison. I mustn't forget: there was also my toothbrush and the scissors with the rounded ends!

An hour or so later I was given an issue of the big German magazine *Signal,* and told it was "to read on the train"! The magazine depicted, of course, mostly the propaganda photographs released by the Germans, although it did mention some Allied achievements as well. All one had to do was to add a good many miles to the Allied advances mentioned, and this would yield an approximate real status. (It turned out the Allies were much closer than I had ever dreamed possible.)

There was no doubt in my mind that it was most urgent that my departure be effected before they discovered that I was not to be included, for I was now a little more than ten days from my execution date.

The noon meal was meted out, but there was no indication of departure. The hours ticked by, and the sirens wailed a couple of times; the Allies' advance must have been tremendously rapid. When the evening pittance was delivered I inquired when departure was scheduled. The young matron lifted her shoulders in a gesture of ignorance.

There was unusual noise coming from the women's cells on the ground floor—lots of loud talk, and even singing at one point. As expected, all this commotion brought on the inevitable reaction from the guard in the courtyard, and his voice thundered with the admonition, *"Ruhe!"* (Silence!)

The next twenty-four hours were no different. At evening mealtime, when my cell door opened, I inquired, *"Wann fahren wir ab?"* (When are we leaving?) *"Ich weiss es nicht!"* (I don't know!) replied the matron, this time in a voice tinted with discouragement. Obviously, our German guards' morale was sinking badly!

I spent those long tedious hours in my cell, mostly sitting at my table catching what I thought were baby bedbugs. I had become quite adept at it, having discovered the method the first week of my incarceration. I sat with my elbows on the table and my hands under my chin, immobile. After a while, I would feel a sharp little prick, and at that spot (generally about a half-inch up my arm) a tiny little pinpoint of bright red would appear. The baby bedbug (an infinitesimal creature) was sucking up my blood. All I had to do was scrape my nail against my skin, bringing the creature down, and squeeze it against the table, dispatching it to its grave!

The third day after the announcement of imminent departure was, in contrast, to the previous couple of days' high level of activity, unusually quiet in the ward. At noon, when my carrot purée was handed to me, I ventured again to inquire about our departure plans, only to receive a short-tempered retort that seemed to contain a mixture of annoyance and worry.

Toward the latter part of the afternoon I heard the cell doors on the lower level being opened; the din of the women's voices grew and grew and became filled with the sounds of laughter, crying. I heard steps along the catwalk coming toward my cell. (I was now, it seemed, the only one left in the solitary confinement section.) This was the moment, no doubt!

The key turned in the keyhole. I was already standing facing the door, pillowcase in hand. My heart was beating furiously. The door opened and the young matron, very sullen, said in a soft voice, *"Zu Hause!"* (Go home!)

I stared at her. I couldn't believe my ears. Finally I uttered, *"Bei mir, zu Hause?"* (To *my* home?) *"Ja, ja. . . ."* she replied in a quiet, subdued voice.

She moved aside and let me pass. I rushed down the little corkscrew staircase, and found myself swallowed up in a mass of screaming, laughing, crying women. One passed out to my right.

We were packed like sardines in that hall. The chief matron ordered *"Ruhe"* (silence), but didn't succeed very well at obtaining compliance; then slowly we started moving forward through the big doors, the first of a series leading toward the exit.

We had advanced about twenty-five to thirty feet inside a second corridor, when the Feldwebel appeared. He seemed beside himself. He was yelling at the matrons, "What do you think you are doing?" and ordered us to back up, back into our ward!

This was a very emotional moment. We had had a glimpse of freedom, and now we were snared in the web again. Fear and despair welled up in all of us, I am sure.

The Feldwebel and his female cohorts had a heated argument, but at the conclusion we were again allowed to proceed forward. The series of doors and corridors were quite familiar to me. I had gone through them many times when I was taken out by Helmer for interrogation.

We were herded one after the other into the German offices near the prison gate. Our belongings were returned: the little money, my wristwatch, etc. I found myself being signed out by the same soldier who had signed me in on the day of my arrest; the one who had been so nice and who, I believe, would have liked to help me get a message out, had he been able to.

I asked him what was going to happen to him now. In a very dejected way he lifted his shoulders, and whispered, *"Ich weiss nicht!"*

6   The prison gate opened, and I found myself alone in the street. Not a soul was in sight. I learned later that people had heard that the Germans were setting the prisoners free, and for most of the

day a crowd had gathered in the street until the Germans pushed them back and ordered the street cleared.

It was about six o'clock. How strange it felt to be free. . . . I still couldn't believe it! I walked briskly toward a square a few blocks away, where I could catch a streetcar. I was embarrassed by my appearance, dressed as I was and carrying that big white pillow case with my prisoner number embroidered on it. I was afraid I might be seen by any acquaintance! How foolish, and how unbelievable my embarrassment seems when looked at now, more than forty years later, from here in America. But at the time, in my native Belgium, class distinctions were very strong. I presented an image that was a far cry from my former well-groomed appearance.

The streetcar stopped, and I jumped on the front platform, where there would be less chance of bumping into someone I knew, and moved into the corner behind the conductor. He turned to me with a warm smile, and said, "Coming out of the 'Big Hotel' too, aren't you?"

The street scene presented some pleasant surprises. German command cars, completely camouflaged with tree branches, rushed through traffic. German trucks, filled with soldiers and materiel and also camouflaged with greenery, headed out of town. What a marvelous sight! They were in retreat! They were on the run!

It was getting dark. I didn't want to go to my apartment yet. What was I going to find there? Had Helmer emptied it of all its contents? I just couldn't face this possibility at that moment. I felt rather drained after all the emotions of the day.

I headed instead for my Uncle César's home. What a haven this was! His warmth, his genuine joy at seeing me safe, felt good. We talked. Even though I was really emotionally exhausted and felt dead tired, I couldn't go to sleep for a long time that night.

The following morning, Uncle César told me that my father had been arrested the same day as I. (A few weeks later I was contacted by a former inmate upon his return from Ravensbruck, a German concentration camp near Berlin. He reported that my father had been murdered by the Germans the night before the camp was liberated by the Russians.)

After breakfast I left to go to my own apartment. From my uncle's home I had to pass right by the Berchem caserne occupied, of course, by the German troops. From there I had to cross the wide "Grande Chaussée," the highway to Brussels.

The Germans had dug trenches all along the area separating the caserne from the Brussels highway. I walked gingerly along these diggings, with a song in my heart. About one hundred feet from the corner, a huge gate-like contraption sat across the whole width of the highway. It was about ten feet high, and seemed set so as to have some mobility. It turned out this was an "anti-tank" gate.

About ten minutes later I opened the front door of the apartment house. Everything was quiet. I went up the two flights of stairs and found myself very apprehensive as I inserted the key in my apartment door.

The first glimpse was shocking. All sorts of items of clothing and personal effects were piled on the floor of the little entrance hall. Most of it had been thrown out of the closet facing the entrance door.

The huge oak buffet (a magnificent piece of furniture, adorned with wood carvings) and full of secret drawers had been raided as well. From it, one of my most prized possessions had been stolen: my worldwide stamp collection, which had been started by my paternal grandfather, passed on to my father, who worked on it for many years, then handed it over to me, who had by now devoted at least twenty years to it. It was invaluable, irreplaceable, but it was gone. Other than that and a small strongbox containing personal documents, most of my belongings were still there, and despite the ransacking my apartment had sustained, I felt relieved.

Suddenly I observed some feverish activity on the street below. A short while previously some German military cars had roared by, camouflaged with tree branches. But now there were Belgian civilians hurrying down the avenue, and they seemed very excited. I rushed down and followed them in the direction of the Grande Chaussée.

Several people were already standing at the corner of the first cross-street, Avenue Reine Elizabeth, one block from the Grande Chaussée. Suddenly there was rifle fire, and at about the same moment, there appeared out of a side street half a block away, two English "Tommies!"

At the sound of the rifle fire we all retreated to the safety of the big entrance way of the corner apartment house, the one that had been occupied by the Germans. From there we watched our first Allied ground troops. Our liberators! They ran toward us in a crouched position across Avenue Royale. A few houses from the corner where we stood had been the German command post. We didn't know if the Germans had vacated it and fled, or if they were still holed up in it.

A British soldier sneaked up to the corner; a man in our group signaled to him, toward the house: a warning signal. A couple more British soldiers appeared in the street half a block away, and followed the same course as their leader. A few more shots rang out. Nothing stirred at the former German command post, and the British soldiers sped across the avenue toward it.

The whole scene suddenly struck me as quite funny. This was real war! We were watching our liberators suddenly appear from nowhere; real bullets were being fired, and we civilians were watching it all from the shelter of the entrance to a big apartment building. It looked as if we were watching little boys playing war!

But the reality of the situation took over, and joy welled up in us. What a sight! Our liberators! What a feeling: freedom from the German yoke!

Another shot was fired: not a rifle shot this time, but a much heavier one. I was back in my apartment by now, and the deflagration sounded quite close. It turned out to be a most dramatic happening.

In the side street, at a house only 150 yards from my apartment, a gentleman elated by the arrival of the British had raised the Belgian flag on the roof of his home to be seen from all around. It was seen, all right, as far as the caserne at the Grande Chaussée, and the Germans, still entrenched there, lobbed a shell, making a direct hit and killing the gentleman. What a horror! After four years of oppression under the heel of the Germans, to be mowed down by them at the precise moment he saw the fulfillment of the four-year-long dream! Liberation!

Events unfurled rapidly. The British troops were entering Antwerp from our side. The anti-tank gates the Germans had set upon the approaches to the caserne just folded over, and the tanks and trucks of our liberators rolled right on. At the same moment, Canadian troops were entering the city from the other side, taking the more direct and newer highway to Brussels.

The Germans were in full retreat.

How can I describe our elation, our gratitude toward our liberators? There are no words to express it. It was like a madness. One wanted to embrace every Allied soldier. We had so little to give, but whatever we had we wanted to share with them. I, for one, told the boys they were welcome any time. My apartment was open to them.

As expected, the fury of the people toward collaborators of the Germans led to some acts of violence. Belgian women who had been lovers of the Germans were rounded up by the populace, who shaved the women's hair off, then paraded them in open trucks through the streets of Antwerp.

The Belgian SS, who had served with the German SS, were also targets of some vengeful acts by the Belgian population. The story goes, for example, that some of those caught in Antwerp were put down in the cells of the SS Headquarters and forced to lick the bloodstains off the whitewashed walls in the cellar—bloodstains left by the Belgian patriots tortured there.

Now that the Allies were in control in town, we, the Resistance, came out in the open. We were also given armbands, depicting our affiliations. We of Group G had a white armband with a small strip of the Belgian national colors stitched on it, and the letter G printed on it. Those of us who, like me, were part of the headquarters of the group, had a wider blue armband with a square showing the Belgian lion stitched in the middle on the Belgian national colors background.

There was much work to do. We had to establish official records as to members injured or killed in the course of duty. The paperwork was quite extensive. Father Leclef (who had been obliged to go into hiding at the time of my arrest), Abbé Mogenet, and myself worked diligently at this task.

Father Leclef was, as I have said before (and I can't repeat it often enough), a marvelous person—so human, so warm, so straight—an exceptional human being. For many years he was a professor at a Catholic college, where he later became an administrator. And after the war he was made chaplain of the naval academy. All through the war he had been active in intelligence. He had been a member of the General Sabotage Group, and had been very active in the Escape Line as well. I repeat, he was an exceptional individual!

Abbé Mogenet was a Jesuit priest whose brother had been one of the first Resistance fighters executed by the Germans. The Abbé had to go in hiding; I don't know the reason. I can only assume it was related to his brother's arrest and execution. He was incognito until the liberation time, hiding at the Colonial University (two blocks away from my home).

On October 21, 1944, I was invited to attend a formal dinner at the residence of Baroness van de Werve de Schilde. She had been a supporter of our Resistance activities throughout the war.

It was a beautiful party. Several Allied officers were among the guests. What a thrill this was, so shortly after the shackles of the German occupation had been broken. It seemed like a dream. Was I really led around the dance floor by this British colonel? Wasn't it a dream, this serious conversation I had with the Royal Air Force wing commander? And the jovial American colonel, wasn't he, too, part of a dream? No! It was real! So real! So wonderful!

There was one sour note—the presence of Mrs. V. If I had only known then what I learned later, I might have taken action there and then. Her betrayal of me at the SS headquarters the first day of my arrest was a crime which could have been attributed to weakness or lack of character; but she had committed another vile act toward the Vereecken family, my neighbors in whose apartment the SS were lying in waiting to arrest me.

After the liberation, rumors were spread about a vile act supposedly committed by me toward the Vereeckens. It turned out that this act, which was of the utmost villainy, had been committed by V. The SS had already had V. in custody, and had brought her into the Vereecken apartment, and she hid incriminating documents in the toilet area, while in their apartment under SS custody. This came to light when she had the audacity to come and claim them after the liberation.

I have a letter from Mrs. Vereecken in which she expressed her shock at hearing that this crime was attributed to me, and wondered what was the origin of these false rumors! She stated that whenever she related the ugly act, she always clearly named the culprit V!

Although Antwerp was liberated on September 4, 1944, we had not exactly been unaware that the battle to crush the Nazis was still going on in full force. The Battle of the Bulge, in the Belgian Ardennes in December, had been fierce. The Germans very nearly succeeded in breaching the American defenses. Had they done so, their push to regain possession of the Port of Antwerp would certainly have been successful.

We were also subjected to ever increasing bombardment by V-1s. The British batteries set up around the city became very accurate at shooting them down. One night it was reported that the count was seventy-eight, or about one-half of the rockets launched toward us during twenty-four hours.

The V-1s were launched from Holland. They were aimed at two targets in Antwerp. From my bedroom window you could clearly see them coming. They were headed either toward the port area, or toward the big parks adjacent to my apartment. The British were using these parks as a big motor pool, as the huge trees offered excellent cover for their vehicles.

One could hear the V-1s coming. They sounded like the rumble of a big truck motor. As long as the rumble continued, one was safe; when it stopped, it meant the contraption was coming down. Then came the big *bang* of the explosion.

The rockets aimed at the park always came right over my block. Every time we heard them, we whispered, "Keep going, keep going. . . ." Then the sudden silence caused us to hold our breath and wait five or six seconds for the *bang*. Maybe we would be the ones to get a direct hit!

One weekend the V-2s hit. This was a new weapon of terrible destructive force. The heavy warhead was rocketed into the stratosphere. It followed a ballistic path at supersonic speed and fell upon its target without any warning sound. Its exploding warhead would flatten an entire city block.

Damage to the city by these two new weapons was tremendous.

May 8, 1945, was a beautiful balmy day.

The news reports of the continued advance of the Allied armies on enemy territory and their relentless bombing of Germany was music to our ears. Victory seemed certain. But was it a question of weeks? Of days?

I had dropped in at my uncle's apartment, and we listened to a news broadcast. It was the historic moment we had been hoping for with more and more fervor: Germany had surrendered.

The elation that welled up in us had no bounds. I bid my uncle goodbye and had an urge to hurry toward the center of town. I felt like dancing all the way down; I felt like singing! This spirit seemed to exude from most of the pedestrians. There was no need to talk, but one could sense everyone's joy; it seemed they all cried out, "The war is over! The war is over!"

I arrived downtown just as the city lights came on for the first time in five years! The enthusiasm of the citizenry exploded. What a magnificent sight, those city lights! After five years of constant blackout! What a welling of gratitude rose in us for the Allies, our wonderful liberators, whose armies had achieved the final blow: the crushing of the Nazi war machine!

1 As soon as we neared the completion of the records, document-
ing the activities, injuries, and losses of Group G, I was in dire
need of a job. My search in the business world of Antwerp was
unproductive. Next I applied at a British military employment
bureau, and landed a job in a steno pool. The job proved quite
unsatisfactory, however. It was tedious work compared to the executive secretary job I had held for about fifteen years, but I needed to
eat and pay my rent. However, my lot improved when shortly
afterward I applied for and got a job as secretary at the American
Quartermaster Section, Headquarters 13th Port.

My social life was quite active. The funny thing was that most of
my social relations were British. Several times a week British
officers would fetch me at the office at the close of the workday for
dinner and dance at the British Officers Club two blocks from my
office. Ironically, my boss's right-hand man, a master sergeant,

strongly disliked the British; every morning after he had seen me leave with the British officers, he would greet me with, "Good morning, Limey lover!" ("Limey" was a derogatory expression for the British.)

The day I was invited to a semi-formal dinner by a British colonel, a medical doctor, I found myself in a quandary. The only dressy shoes I had were of black silk. But they were worn; the silk had cracked, and showed the underlying white base. Fortunately, my four years of ingenuity came to the fore, and I proceeded to brush black ink all over the flaws. The result was perfect: not the slightest fissure showed. With this crisis taken care of, I had a delightful evening.

When it was time to go home we found ourselves facing a downpour. Rain was coming down in buckets. My escort hailed several military cars, but in vain. By now we were both soaked. But it was a balmy night, so what harm could such a drenching do? The situation we found ourselves in, without transportation, was so incongruous. My escort felt guilty and kept apologizing despite my reassurances.

We finally got some transportation, and twenty minutes later I was back in my apartment. Every step I made was accompanied by a squishing sound! My shoes were soaking wet. What a sight when I took them off! The ink I had used to camouflage the wear on my shoes had run, permeating my stockings and, more disastrously, my feet! The toes and the skin between them were impregnated with the black ink! It took me two weeks, at least, to remove it! So much for my brainstorm!

As soon as the war was over, I was awarded two decorations. The first came very shortly after the liberation. I was invited to come to the city hall in Berchem, a suburb of Antwerp. There to my surprise, a ceremony was held in my honor, and a bronze medal was awarded me by the Fédération Nationale des Décorés pour Actes de Courage et Dévouement (National Federation of Decorated Individuals for Acts of Courage and Self-Sacrifice).

The War Office

LONDON.

          The Supreme Headquarters of the Allied
Expeditionary Force have decided to present three
hundred and fifteen certificates to Belgian
Resistants in recognition of the exceptional service
rendered by them to the Allied cause, which greatly
assisted the invasion of Europe and the course of
the battles which followed.

          Your name was among those brought to the
attention of the War Office as having played an
important part in the liberation of Belgium and I
have, therefore, the honour to send you the enclosed
certificate.

          In order that the register of names may be
kept up to date, I would ask you to sign and return
the enclosed receipt to the British Embassy, Brussels.
The completed register of names will then be sent to
the Ministere de la Defense Nationale for their records.
I would add that the number on your certificate has no
connection with the order of merit.

          On behalf of His Brittanic Majesty's
Government, I congratulate you and thank you for
your contribution to the victory of the United
Nations.

Major-General

Letter from the War Office in London forwarding the SHAEF certificate

A couple of months later I had received a certificate of merit from SHAEF (Supreme Headquarters Allied Expeditionary Force) signed by General Dwight D. Eisenhower, Supreme Commander. (The certificate, reproduced herewith, bears my maiden and first married names; it was, the reader will note, prepared for male recipients.)

One morning two British officers appeared at my office and identified themselves to my boss, Major Meiser. He seemed very upset and clearly resentful of whatever they were telling him. I

The name of
Madame Judels-de-Ridder
has been placed on record at
The Supreme Headquarters
Allied Expeditionary Force
as being commended for brave
conduct while acting under my
orders in the liberation of his
country 1944 – 45

Dwight D Eisenhower
Supreme Commander

The SHAEF Certificate

realized from what I overheard that it concerned me. One of the major's protestations was, "Do you know this girl has been decorated, and holds a certificate of merit signed by General Eisenhower?"

This visit was the beginning of one of the most painful series of events that ever happened to me. These officers were coming for me. I was driven to their headquarters, and a few minutes later invited into one of the offices. The British officer seated behind the desk asked me a series of questions relating, of course, to my Resistance activities. I had no inkling of what they needed me for, but if I could be of help, I would be only too glad.

But after a while, the questioning took a slant that I resented. There seemed to be more and more the tone of suspicion. I was appalled.

I tried to keep my mounting anger in check. I realized rather quickly that the suspicion was due to the fact that I had worked in association with Donald who turned out to be a double agent and who, no doubt, was the one who turned me in to the Germans.

The hours ticked by, and at noon I was invited to join the officers in the dining room for lunch. There was a long table at which at least ten or twelve officers were seated. From time to time one would address a few words to me, but the eyes that were otherwise fixed upon me were not exactly belligerent, but definitely inquisitive and suspicious.

After lunch the interrogation started anew. The questions seemed to contain more and more outright belligerence, and only vaguely muted accusations of collaboration with the enemy. My anger grew. I reminded the officer of the hell I had endured while a prisoner of the Germans; of my condemnation to be hanged by them. I expressed my revulsion at the treatment to which I was now subjected. Was this why I had risked my life daily for close to four years?

After a couple of more attempts to question the veracity of my detailed explanations, I suddenly blew up, and slamming my fist on the desk, I shouted, "If you don't believe me, why don't you ask X!"

The officer stared at me intently, excused himself, and left his office. I was fuming! ("X," whose name I had thrown at him, was the British agent mentioned before, whom I had worked with and who had delighted me so much by visiting me with François at the hideout.)

I was still fuming when the officer reappeared, accompanied by another. Standing at the desk, the one who had been grilling me spoke: "We are very sorry; this was all a terrible mistake!"

The genuine tone of the apology was a relief, but it took me a long time to recover from this experience. As a matter of fact, two years later, while working for the American forces in Germany, there was a painful sequel to this, one I was never able to redress.

I was in the American officers' club having cocktails with some of them, when some Britishers—three, I think—walked in. We started conversing; I probably reiterated my gratitude to them for liberating my hometown, Antwerp. We were having a delightful time until, a short time later, another British officer joined them. He seemed familiar to me. I never forget a face, nor the sound of a voice. He stared at me, and I mentioned that I seemed to recognize him. He didn't respond to my query. A few minutes later after he had been talking to his three compatriots, they all moved away. I saw them again a couple of days later, and they avoided me.

Then it dawned on me: the one who looked familiar had been at the luncheon table that horrible day in Antwerp. He had never been told that they had made a terrible mistake in suspecting me. All he knew was that I had been brought in there that day, suspected of being a German collaborator!

I liked working at headquarters 13th port, even though the job was quite different from the heavy load of responsibilities I had carried for fourteen years in my father's office. The pay was good, too.

In the civilian world outside the office, however, things were going on I didn't like at all. More precisely, it was the constant and blatant whitewashing of collaborators. Furthermore, the ranks of Resistance fighters grew at a tremendous speed. The supposed resistants were coming out in droves. It seemed every second citizen of Antwerp belonged to the AS (Armée Secrète), one of the Resistance groups, and their armbands were seen everywhere. It appeared that anything qualified a person to claim to be a Resistant or *Weerstander!* To have smuggled some potatoes from a field outside the city; to have thumbed one's nose at the Germans, etc.

We at Group G had a tangible example of whitewashing. Right after the liberation, we were using a car to drive our commandant around with his bodyguards. (We had to be careful for sniper attacks by pro-Germans, who were still around.) The car was a big black Cord—a pretentious car—which had been requisitioned. It had belonged to a citizen who had trafficked with the Germans and done big business with the enemy. Obviously, the individual had quite some influence, for in a short time the car was ordered returned to him; just one example of the many injustices we saw, the number of which grew at a tremendous rate. It was revolting to see profiteers—those who had cashed in on their collaboration with the enemy—freed from prosecution and free to profit from their ill-earned wealth.

On the other hand, some of us who had risked our lives daily for the cause of liberation found ourselves under attack by some elements; there were derogatory remarks, smear campaigns, and outright lies aiming at character assassination. I personally found myself the victim of such a campaign. A nosy neighbor had surveyed the comings and goings at my home, and, having seen nothing but men (including Father Leclef) entering and leaving at all hours, branded me in a report. She also notified the college where Father Leclef was an administrator of his "frequenting a woman of ill-repute"! She had to eat her words shortly afterwards, when the true facts of our patriotic activities became known!

Another personal attack—vile to the highest degree—came from an official of an institute of learning who had propositioned me during my visit to his office on Resistance business (he was involved in Resistance as well). I rejected his advances, and he took his revenge by spreading the most damaging lies about me. It took an official letter from the "big boss" of Group G to squelch these rumors. The "big boss" was as outraged about the smears as I was, and the terms employed in his official letter left no doubt about it!

Disillusion and disgust welled up in me. So, when the American forces announced they were looking for secretaries to work for them in Germany, I applied for a job.

2 In March of 1946 I was on my way to Germany as a result of my application for a transfer to the American zone of occupation. Having been occupied by the Nazis for four years, this was my opportunity to return the courtesy!

The tedious series of formalities required to obtain all the necessary official documents from the Belgian authorities was the first step. Bureaucracy works slowly. Despite my decorations and the certificate of merit from SHAEF, the bureaucratic wheels turned slowly. But, finally, at end of March, 1946, I left Antwerp by train for Frankfurt am Main, via Paris.

I found myself assigned to the TI&E (Troop Information and Education) Staff School, as a secretary to the commandant. The whole TI&E was located in Höchst, about eight miles from Frankfurt. The offices were set up in what had been an I.G. Farben dye factory.

Once again I had to undergo what was, for me, a dreaded experience: the questioning of my capabilities. I was interviewed by Sgt. Balsley, a career Army woman who was to become my immediate superior. She was older than I, and appeared cold and thorough. I soon found out, however, that underneath her cold military appearance she was a very lovely person. She didn't allow any nonsense, however, for which I admired her even more.

A long time later she told me what had impressed her very much on my first day at TI&E. I had been sitting at my desk, putting things in order and waiting for my first assignment. One of my first concerns was the condition of my typewriter, and I thoroughly cleaned its type, roller, etc. This to her was a very good sign in my favor!

I enjoyed my way of life, even though it was so new and different. I was billeted in one of the German apartment houses, fifteen minutes' walk from work. It was a three-story building in which several girls shared an apartment; each had her own bedroom, but there was only one bathroom for all. We took our meals in the mess hall at the officers' club in the building across the street from the office. I was often invited for cocktails before dinner by the officers. It was there in the officers' club that I was indoctrinated in the consumption of martinis! My association with the group of officers of TI&E was most pleasant.

On June 5, 1946, TI&E took a field trip on the Rhine aboard Hitler's yacht. The yacht, called *Stadt Köln* (City of Cologne), was presented to Adolf Hitler by the city of Cologne in 1938, at a cost of one million reichsmark equal then to about $400,000 dollars. The yacht was about 180 feet long by 24 feet wide. In one of the rooms one wall was covered with a map of Germany made entirely of inlaid wood of excellent workmanship, showing the different regions and activities of Germany: agriculture, industry, etc. The yacht was now under the control of the Chief of Transporation of USFET (United States Forces European Theater).

Several miles from Frankfurt, in the Taunus Mountains, was Kronberg Castle, residence of the Princess of Hesse, a beautiful, majestic place. The castle—its real name is "Schloss Friedrichs-

Entrance to Kronberg Castle

Terrace side of Kronberg Castle (reproduced from The Stars and Stripes)

hof'—was designed by the court architect for Kaiserin Friedrich, widow of Emperor Friedrich of Germany and daughter of Queen Victoria of England. She had the castle built during the years of 1888–92, after the death of her husband.

The Empress died in 1901 and left the castle to her youngest daughter (Landgraefin von Hesse). She and her family made the castle their summer residence until 1920, when it was occupied by French troops; she then took residence in the fifteen-room cottage within the park. The U.S. Army took possession of the castle in May, 1945, and it was then used as a club for officers of the rank of colonel and above.

The atmosphere of the castle was magnificent. Only American and Allied guests of the high-ranking officers were allowed. As we entered the hall we were greeted by an M.P. in polished helmet and white gloves. The officers had to sign the register. A year or so later, all ranks of officers were allowed. Later there was even more relaxation on the rules, and soon officers were allowed to bring German girls as their guests. The big entrance hall contained a huge fireplace, where huge logs burned profusely. It was so special to sit there sipping a cocktail before dinner.

The original furniture still adorned the salons. The dining room was beautiful with its high-backed chairs, and impeccable service

Queen Victoria's portrait in the dining room, Kronberg Castle

was rendered by the maître d'—in white tie and tails—who seemed to be an integral part of the surroundings. The quietness that reigned there added to the majestic aura of the place.

I dined there many a time under the watchful eye of a portrait of Queen Victoria of England! The beautiful life-size oil painting of the monarch, artistically lit, showed her in profile, in a black dress, hands folded in her lap, with a black mantilla draped over her head and shoulders.

After dinner we moved to one of the salons, where a five- or six-piece orchestra played beautiful ballroom music. I have wonderful memories of the many evenings I spent there.

I was given a pass to go to Belgium, where I was to attend a ceremony at which I was to be presented with another medal, the Group G Bronze Medal.

The author in military uniform

I arrived from Germany in uniform. We Allies working in the American zone of occupation in Germany were authorized to wear the American uniform with a patch on the sleeve, just below the shoulder, indicating our country of origin. Thus I wore the patch "Belgium."

At the ceremony, when my name was called, a Belgian general presented me with the decoration and proceeded to pin it to my uniform. Perhaps because of the solid weave of the uniform material, or because of dullness of the pin, the poor man tried repeatedly to pin the medal on, but without success. The situation became practically embarrassing, but luckily the two pins finally penetrated the material, and we both let out a sigh of relief!

Soon after my return to Germany, I was again revolted by some underhanded manipulations by my new immediate superior, and I requested a transfer. I had been with the Staff School since March, 1946; it was now August, 1947, and I was stationed in Bamberg.

As it happened, the Chief of Unit Publications, Captain Wright, had asked me for quite some time to work with him as his executive secretary, but I had turned him down. I contacted him now, inquiring whether he was still interested in my working for him. The answer was an enthusiastic "Yes."

A couple of days later, despite the insistence of my present boss that I reconsider, I stood my ground and was granted permission to transfer.

About six months later, the whole TI&E was on the move again. We had been in Bamberg barely six months.

The author at her desk in civilian clothes

Our new destination was Stuttgart. We worked and were billeted in the Möhringen Caserne, surrounded by beautiful woods. From the window of my room on the second floor, I could almost touch the branches of the trees.

It was a wonderful location as far as I was concerned, although some of the British girls complained bitterly, especially because the new TI&E commandant forbade entertainment in the women's quarters. No male visitors were allowed. There were some who found a way around this order, though, despite the DP (displaced person) guard posted at the entrance to our billets!

The officers' club in Stuttgart itself was very nice, and provided us with a pleasant dancing facility.

One of my big pleasures in Stuttgart was to go for a walk through the woods after work. Unfortunately, after an unpleasant experience, I had to forego it. One beautiful autumn afternoon I went on my customary stroll. The weather was balmy; some low sunrays still shone through the branches. Suddenly I had a pang of anxiety; I couldn't put my finger on what exactly it was that alerted me to some danger. I have tremendously sharp hearing, and a keen awareness of my surroundings wherever I am. Was it an unusual rustling or crackling I had heard? Whatever it was, my senses were definitely on the alert.

I accelerated my stride, and then I detected the reason for my alarm. I heard crackling over the leaf-strewn ground, in unison with my stride. I stopped abruptly; it stopped. No doubt, I was being followed! I didn't hesitate, but took off running as fast as I could. I reached the security of the Caserne safely, but this put an unfortunate end to my lovely solitary walks through the woods!

I came back from a long weekend pass to Antwerp to find my office cleared of its files, and I was greeted with the announcement that the Unit Publications section of TI&E had been transferred to Pfungstadt (near Darmstadt), where the *Stars and Stripes,* the military newspaper, was located. I was to move up there immediately. I was devastated to have to leave this wonderful location. Nevertheless, a

The author at work in Unit Publications,
Pfungstadt, Germany

footlocker containing all my belongings was put on a jeep, and off I went with a driver, to my new home.

What a shock it was at first! Pfungstadt was a little village that looked very dismal. It had rained, mud was everywhere. Oh! how I missed already the beautiful woods surrounding the Möhringen Caserne near Stuttgart!

I met my new boss, an American civilian named Jack Browne, who had previously been on the staff of the *Stars and Stripes*. He was a very nice person.

I moved into my new quarters: a private home shared by five girls, four of whom were on the *Stars and Stripes* staff, and myself. I was

An article that appeared in Stars and Stripes, *December 1948*

Friday, December 31, 1948   THE STARS AND STRIPES

Two More Medals

Yvonne De Ridder
.. Sten guns, grenades and dynamite

Belgian Girl Gets 7th Medal For Her Part in Resistance

PFUNGSTADT, Dec. 30 (S&S)—A Belgian priest and former resistance group commander came to Pfungstadt, bringing two medals for bravery to Yvonne de Ridder, of Antwerp, from the Belgian government.

Miss De Ridder, a Department of the Army civilian, now works for EUCOM Unit Publications under the direction of *The Stars and Stripes.* Her Medal of Resistance and the Commemorative Medal from the Belgian minister of national defense brought to a total of seven her awards for exceptional bravery in her country's resistance movement.

As a member of a sabotage group from 1941–45 she kept Sten guns, grenades and dynamite in the cellar of her home. She ran a boarding house for Allied aviators who had bailed out over Belgium and transported munitions for the men of Resistance Group G. Miss De Ridder has been decorated by Belgium, the U.S. and three times by France. Her U.S. Certificate of Merit was signed by Gen Dwight D. Eisenhower, commending her for "brave conduct while acting under my orders in the liberation of her country."

From 1941 she helped send information to England on German installations and troop movements. She was later denounced by a Nazi agent who had infiltrated the resistance forces.

assigned a room on the second floor; it had a balcony surrounded by vines. Here is where I rushed at lunch time and where, on sunny days, I sunbathed every minute available!

There was very little social activity here. There was lots of card playing at the Château Meaux, the club and mess of *Stars and Stripes,* and of course the bar at the club was very popular.

In December 1948, I had the great pleasure of a visit from Father Leclef, my dear friend from the Belgian Resistance. He brought me two medals that had been bestowed upon me by the Belgian government: the *Médaille de la Résistance* (Resistance Medal) and the *Commemorative de la Guerre 1940–45* (Commemorative of the War 1940–45). The latter bore two crossed sabers for "action," and the two lightning bolts for "intelligence" action was, of course, for sabotage.

These were my third and fourth medals from Belgium. I had also by now been awarded the French Commemorative with *Barrette "Liberation,"* and two medals from the Réseau Lord Denys (French Intelligence)—The Resistance Medal and the *Officier Dévouement Social.*

3 In mid-1948, at one of the *Stars and Stripes* parties, I met a newcomer to the staff, an American journalist from California with whom I danced often that evening. He was a very good dancer. A romance ensued, and the next year we were married at the city hall of Pfungstadt by the mayor himself, and set up house in Darmstadt, not far from the office.

In 1950 we came to the United States on a two-month vacation. We landed in New York on July 31, and forty-eight hours later were in Washington, D.C., trying to put in motion the formalities for my American citizenship. (My husband was on leave, having signed a new two-year contract with *Stars and Stripes*; therefore, I, as an Allied wife of a U.S. citizen employed by the American government or para-government agency in Germany, could apply for citizenship the moment I set foot on American soil.) We were sent from pillar to post all day, from one office to the other. Finally, toward the close of the day, I was asked if I could appear the following day at 1 P.M. with two witnesses, and be ready to undergo the examination. The gentleman told me where I could get a booklet (which turned out to have, I think, 128 pages) to help me! I was in shock! I had made notes before leaving Germany with the idea of studying them for two months in the United States. Now I had less than twenty-four hours to digest the intricacies of the U.S. government, its political parties, etc.

I appeared at the prescribed time with two witnesses, friends of my husband. Before my ordeal started, I promised myself to answer all questions directly and succinctly, without volunteering any supplementary details!

I was asked seven or eight questions, all pertaining to the mechanics of U.S. Government, and I rattled off the answers. My interrogator paused, stared at me, then concluded my ordeal by stating, "You seem to know the answers, don't you?"

Before leaving Germany we had ordered a car from Detroit. My husband's brother had taken delivery of it, and now all three of us were off for a drive across the United States, destination: California.

We first went north, toward Montréal, and stopped on the way in Saratoga. This was my first experience at a race track. On the way I had been told how to choose a horse, and how to evaluate its chances (based on the weight carried, the distance covered, the condition of track, etc.). This was all new to me. Both men were experienced at the game; but in the end, who came out ahead—and by over seven dollars? I did! They both lost!

In Canada I had the tremendous pleasure of having a short visit with Charles Shierlaw, one of the Canadian flyers I had sheltered during the war. We had stopped at a hotel Charles had recommended to us. Charles was on vacation himself in that part of Canada. I inquired about him at the desk before going up to our room. The clerk said he had not registered yet. Rather disappointed because we had arrived quite a bit later than planned, and expected him to be there by now, we went up to our rooms.

A long corridor, narrow and rather dimly lit, led to our rooms. A tall gentleman was walking toward us. I glanced at him as he passed me by, and abruptly turned around and faced him. He had also whirled around, and "Chas!" "Yvonne!" we blurted from our respective mouths!

What an emotional moment this was for me! How vivid our last goodbye still was in my mind, that June afternoon when we were under surveillance and Donald came to take Charles away.

The next day we pushed on toward California. I remember being astonished by the configuration of the innumerable little towns we drove through on our journey. Single-story buildings lined the "main" streets (sometimes the only street). And all the store windows were filled with horribly big advertisements. It was quite a contrast to Europe where storefronts were generally made as attractive as possible, offering the wares in orderly, attractive displays. To this day I am appalled at this lack of visual appeal!

California, and especially southern California, looked magnificent to me: the "eternal" sunshine, the greenery, the flowers, the mountains, the beach, the desert, the architecture . . . "Heaven on earth" I called it.

By the end of August or early September we were heading back east, taking the southern route this time. All during my vacation I had worried about the second exam for my citizenship. When I had successfully completed the first exam, the agent in Washington had told me that the second one would be in public, in front of a judge. I had lived these two months with the fear of publicly failing an oral exam, of making a fool of myself with erroneous answers. It turned out, of course, that my fears had been unfounded, and that the agent had really played a dirty trick on me. The second "exam" was the official swearing-in ceremony, the granting of U.S. citizenship!

I obtained my American citizenship in Washington, D.C., on

September 16, 1950, and received my American passport on September 18. A few days later we sailed back to Europe from New York on the ship *De Grasse,* for a final two years with the American forces in Germany.

A couple of months after our return to Darmstadt, I had to undergo major surgery. First I went through about three weeks of preliminary tests at 97th General Hospital in Frankfurt; then came the operation, and a few days later I was back home for a few more days of recuperation, then went back to work.

Very soon my husband was assigned to a new job at *Stars and Stripes,* and we transferred to an apartment in Frankfurt on the corner of Kalle Strasse, overlooking the grounds of the IG Farben building.

I had quit my job; this was the first time in over twenty-one years that I was a lady of leisure; no more dictation, no more typewriter, no more filing, no more office work! Instead, I enjoyed playing the piano and playing tennis. The Press Club was close by, a mere fifteen minutes' brisk walk. It had been set up in a private residence surrounded by nice grounds, including two tennis courts. The news media, including reporters for Associated Press, United Press, other agencies, and other *Stars and Stripes* bureau chiefs would congregate there at day's end. The cocktail hours were always interesting and lively. I enjoyed many social hours there following vigorous workouts on the tennis courts.

4 We returned to the United States toward the end of 1952 and took up residence in the Los Angeles area during the first part of 1953.

In December, 1954, I received an invitation from the British Embassy to come to Washington to accept King George's Medal for Courage in the Cause of Freedom, bestowed upon me by the Queen of England. If I were unable to come to Washington, the medal would be given to me by the consul general of Great Britain in Los Angeles.

<u>Madame Yvonne Sadi Josephine Frédérique De Ridder</u>
<u>King's Medal for Courage in the Cause of Freedom</u>

<u>CITATION</u>

Madame De Ridder joined the Resistance in the
beginning of 1941 and proved herself to be a member
of the highest value. She showed utter contempt for
danger and never refused any task assigned to her.
She lodged in her own home various Allied pilots.
She was denounced and arrested in July 1944; but
liberated in September of that year. At the time of
her arrest, in spite of savage treatment at the hands
of the Germans, she kept silence and thus saved the
life of several members of her Group.

My husband declared the trip to Washington would be too
expensive, and that I should accept it in Los Angeles.

It was a very impressive ceremony. The press, the radio, and
television were all there.

The King George's Medal, I was told, was the highest medal
awarded a civilian for combat-related activities during wartime. This
big honor gave rise to another event.

Ralph Edwards, the producer of the show, "This Is Your Life"
read the article about my receiving the decoration, and immediately
put the wheels in motion to have me as his subject on his show.

I was new in America; I didn't have a television; I had never seen
"This Is Your Life."

Ralph Edwards was very strict about secrecy. No leaks could
occur; the subject had to be completely unaware of what was about
to happen. I won't divulge how he managed to achieve this, or what

Reunion on "This Is Your Life": (from left) Louis Rabinowitz,
Leslie Anderson, the author, Father Leclef, and Charles Shierlaw.

use he used to get me to the theater; but on February 23, 1955, less
than three weeks after receiving the King George's Medal, I found
myself called out of an audience at the El Capitan Theater in
Hollywood, brought up on the stage, and during the next half-hour
my life story—especially my wartime activities—were all laid out.
To top it all off, I had the emotional and joyful surprise of being
reunited with three of the flyers I had hidden in my home during the
German occupation of Belgium! They were Louis Rabinowitz from
the United States, Leslie Anderson, and Charles Shierlaw from
Canada. Lastly and most wonderful of all, I was reunited with Father
René Leclef, my fellow Resistance fighter and very dear friend.

It took me at least six months to recover from this event! Wherever I
went, I was recognized and greeted with an enthusiastic "You were on
'This Is Your Life,' " and the person or persons would proceed to
recount details of my life that had been told the night of the show! Even
some six years later, people remembered the show. After work one
evening I was making some purchases at a department store. It was

Author with Alderman Carl Lebon at reception,
Antwerp City Hall, October 27, 1958

about 9 P.M., nearly closing time. A lady accompanied by a little girl was looking through some lingerie items; I had noticed her inquisitive stares at me. Suddenly the words I had heard so often before were spoken: "You were on 'This Is Your Life!'" I acknowledged that this was so, but added, "That was a long time ago!" Then the lady started narrating details that had been divulged during the show!

The "This Is Your Life" show was a real climax in my life, and gave me the excitement of reliving the incidents of wartime service!

In 1958 I returned for a visit to my native Belgium, and was honored at a reception at Antwep city hall.

169

The author and her husband, Lt. Colonel Roger Files

Epilogue

In 1963 my divorce, the procedures of which had been started two years earlier, was finalized.

That same year, in June, the Belgian Government bestowed upon me one more medal, the Civic Cross.

In 1970 I remarried, and with my husband, Lt. Colonel Roger Files—a highly decorated World War II American Air Force fighter pilot—went to Alaska for his last tour of duty before retirement after thirty-five years of service.

We nickname our home in the Santa Monica mountains (forty minutes' drive from downtown Los Angeles) our "Top of the Mountain Retreat." There we enjoy retirement to the fullest!